KITCHEN LIBRARY

THAI
COOKING

KITCHEN LIBRARY

THAI COOKING

Deh-Ta Hsung
Hilaire Walden

GREENWICH
EDITIONS

This edition published in 2005
by Greenwich Editions
The Chrysalis Building
Bramley Road, London W10 6SP

An imprint of **Chrysalis** Books Group plc

All correspondence concerning the content of this
volume should be addressed to Greenwich Editions.

Photographer: Andrew Sydenham
Food stylist: Sue Spaull
Nutritional information: Jenny McGlyne
Editor: Shaun Barrington
Designer: Cara Hamilton
Reproduction: Anorax Imaging Ltd
Printed and bound in China

ISBN 0-86288-810-7

10 9 8 7 6 5 4 3 2 1

Contents

Visual Index

Green Onion Brushes Pretty onion 'trees' suitable as garnish for many recipes p29

Chilli Flowers Deseeded chillies that open up into flowers in cold water p30

Banana Leaf Cups Natural containers for steamed foods that impart their own flavour p31

Carrot Flowers Small and delicate carrot garnishes, best in 'bouquet' clusters p33

Green Curry Paste Green chillies, coriander and lime leaves impart the colour p35

Red Curry Paste Red chillies for the colour, but this also includes coriander and galangal p37

Fragrant Curry Paste Less chillies than green or red curry paste and lime peel for delicate flavour p38

Dipping Sauce 1 Tamarind water, palm sugar, fish sauce, garlic and chilli p41

Dipping Sauce 2 Lime juice, palm sugar, fish sauce and red and green chillies p43

Nam Prik Famous dip for vegetables with dried shrimp, lime juice and chillies p44

Spicy Fish Sauce Piquant fish sauce with chillies, lime juice, sugar and garlic p47

Vegetarian Dipping Sauce Roasted peanuts with chilli sauce and extra chillies p49

Roasted Nam Prik Variation on the classic, with grilled chillies, shrimp paste and peanuts p50

Lemon Grass Soup Light and fresh, with shrimp, fish stock, lemon grass, lime leaves p53

Vermicelli Soup Clear vermicelli, lemon grass, galangal, chillies, garlic p54

Chicken & Mushroom Soup Chicken, Chinese black mushrooms, fish sauce, garlic p56

Pork & Peanut Soup Coriander roots, pork, peanuts, Chinese black mushrooms, bamboo shoots p59

Chicken & Coconut Soup Chicken breast, coconut milk, lemon grass, chillies and lime juice for a visually surprising treat p60

Seafood Soup Squid, scallops and prawns with bean sprouts and cucumber p63

Papaya & Pork Soup Great combination of pork chops and papaya, with fish sauce p65

Gold Bags Prawns, water chestnuts, onions, won-ton skins for deep-fried surprise packages p66

Corn Cakes Sweetcorn, green curry paste, rice flour, cucumber and roasted peanuts p69

Stuffed Chicken Wings Chicken wings, ground pork, prawns, onions, garlic, rice flour p71

Steamed Eggs Smooth blend of eggs, prawns, chillies, coriander leaves, coconut milk p72

Stuffed Eggs Traditional filling of ground pork, prawns, fish sauce, garlic, coriander leaves p73

Egg Nests Delicate parcels of pork, prawns, fish sauce, chillies, coriander leaves p74

Son-In-Law Eggs Golden eggs, onion, fish sauce, palm sugar, red chilli p77

Pork & Noodle Balls Little cages of minced pork, thread noodles, coriander roots, egg p79

Pork Toasts Fingers of minced pork, prawns, garlic, spring onions, eggs, coconut milk p80

Sesame Prawn Toasts Possible party nibbles of prawns, garlic, egg, onion, ginger, sesame seeds p82

Steamed Tofu & Fish Sauce Minced pork, tofu, spring onions, sesame oil, fish sauce p83

Stuffed Omelette Eggs, pork, long or green beans, coriander roots, fish sauce p84

Steamed Crab Subtle mix of crabmeat, pork, shallot, coriander, coconut cream, p86

Stuffed Courgettes Green combo of coriander, courgettes, coconut, lime juice, palm sugar p89

Crab Rolls Chicken, crabmeat, bean sprouts, rice paper wrappers, holy basil leaves p91

Steamed Fish Choice of whole fish such as sea bass or grouper, ginger, sesame and black bean sauce p93

Fried Fish Fillet Choice of firm white fish such as cod, haddock or monkfish, bite-size in batter p94

Fish with Galangal Balls of firm white fish such as halibut or cod, galangal, lemon grass p97

Fish with Lemon Grass Aromatic flatfish such as sole or flounder, lemon grass, chillies, p99

Fish with Coriander & Garlic Fish fillets such as trout or flounder, coriander roots, garlic p101

Fish with Mushroom Sauce Choice of flatfish such as sole or flounder, ginger root, shiitake mushrooms p102

Fish in Coconut Sauce White fish fillets such as red snapper, galangal, steamed in coconut milk p105

Fish with Tamarind & Ginger Whole fish such as bass, ginger root, tamarind water p106

Fish with Chilli Sauce Choice of flatfish such as pomfret or plaice, dried chillies, tamarind water p108

Fish in Banana Leaf Cups Firm white fish such as hake, prawns, peanuts, Chinese cabbage p110

Barbecued Prawns Prawns, onions, chillies, peanuts, served with spicy fish sauce p111

Stir-Fried Prawns Classic stir-fry of prawns, straw mushrooms, water chestnuts, fish sauce p112

Prawns with Lemon Grass Tomatoes, oyster sauce, prawns, lemon grass, coriander p115

Prawns in Yellow Sauce Large prawns, galangal and distinctive turmeric taste and colour p117

Prawns with Garlic Large prawns, ginger root, coriander, garlic, fish sauce p118

Deep-Fried Coconut Prawns King prawns, shredded coconut and coconut milk for the batter p121

Stir-Fried Prawns & Ginger Large prawns, ginger root, fish sauce, spring onions p122

Scallops with Lime Sweet and sharp scallops with galangal, palm sugar, chillies, lime juice p124

Prawns with Mushrooms Large prawns, shiitake mushrooms, lemon grass, dried chilli p126

Mussels with Basil Southeast Asian moules, with Thai basil, galangal, lemon grass p129

Prawn & Cucumber Curry Large prawns, coconut cream, red curry paste, cucumber p130

Squid with Spicy Chillies Fresh squid, root ginger, small red chillies, fish sauce p133

Seafood Skewers Scallops, prawns, white fish fillets, peppers, white wine or sherry p135

Spicy Crab Crabmeat, root ginger, lemon grass, coconut milk, chilli sauce p136

Stuffed Squid Number of baby squid, black fungus, minced pork, vermicelli p138

Duck Curry Succulent duck pieces, prawns, coconut cream and milk, cucumber, palm sugar p141

Chicken in Coconut Milk Tender chicken, coriander roots, coconut milk, lime leaves p142

Chicken with Coriander Spicy chicken drumsticks or thighs, coriander sprigs p144

Lemon Grass Chicken Curry Complex taste amalgam of curry, lemon grass, lime leaves p147

Barbecued Chicken Chicken breasts, coconut cream, tamarind water p148

Spiced Chicken Chicken legs, coriander roots, ginger root, lemon grass, chillies, tamarind water p149

Chicken with Basil Chicken breasts, fresh red chillies, coconut milk, Thai basil leaves p151

Chicken with Galangal Chicken breasts, galangal, Chinese black mushrooms, Thai mint leaves p153

Chicken in Peanut Sauce mildly curried chicken, coconut milk and cream, roasted peanuts p154

Chicken with Mangetout Finely chopped chicken, mangetout, ground browned rice p156

Steamed Chicken Curry Fragrant chicken breasts, lime leaves, curry paste p159

Chicken with Lemon Grass Chicken pieces, green and red chillies, lemon grass p160

Beef Curry Lean beef, red curry paste, long beans or green beans, Chinese black mushrooms p163

Pork with Water Chestnuts Peppery lean pork, water chestnuts, red chillies, coriander p165

Spicy Pork & Lemon Grass Pork fillet, celery, straw mushrooms, lemon grass p166

Barbecued Spare Ribs Pork spare ribs, green curry paste, coconut milk p168

Pork & Bean Stir-Fry Quick meal of pork, long beans or green beans, water chestnuts, prawns p170

Thai Pork Curry Lean diced pork, fragrant curry paste, Thai basil leaves p173

Pork Satay Lean pork, lemon grass, peanuts, red chillies, fish paste, coconut milk p175

Pork & Bamboo Shoots Finely chopped pork, crunchy bamboo shoots and peanuts p176

Vegetables & Pork mixed vegetables such as courgettes, mangetout, chopped pork p179

Pork with Spring Onions Pork, coconut cream, peanuts, galangal, lemon grass, spinach p180

Noodles, Pork & Prawns Thread noodles, prawns, Chinese black mushrooms, pork, celery p183

Crispy Noodles Rice vermicelli, pork, chicken, prawns, bean sprouts with egg 'tears' p184

Thai Fried Noodles Classic, simple dish of rice vermicelli, prawns, dried shrimp, bean sprouts p187

Noodles with Herb Sauce Simple but subtle dish of noodles, Thai basil, Thai mint, coriander p188

Noodles, Crab & Aubergine Brown and white crabmeat, thread noodles, aubergine p191

Noodles with Broccoli Wet rice noodles, pork, roasted peanuts, broccoli p193

Rice, Prawn & Bean Curd
'Fragrant' long-grain white rice, cubed bean curd, prawns p194

Spicy Fried Rice 'Fragrant' long-grain white rice, red curry paste, pork, prawns p197

Thai Fried Rice 'Fragrant' long-grain white rice, pork, chicken, with gorgeous Nam Prik p199

Rice, Chicken & Mushrooms
Long-grain white rice, chicken, Chinese black mushrooms p200

Stuffed Aubergine Boats of chicken breasts, aubergines lemon grass, Thai basil leaves p203

Stir-Fried Mangetout Finely chopped pork, mangetout, prawns, palm sugar p204

Broccoli with Prawns Peanut oil, prawns, broccoli, fish sauce, palm sugar p206

Spiced Cabbage Finely chopped lean pork, white cabbage, coconut cream p208

Vegetables with Sauce
Aubergine, cauliflower, long beans or green beans, coconut milk p209

Mushrooms & Bean Sprouts
Shiitake mushrooms, bean sprouts, prawns, ground browned rice p211

Tossed Spinach Chicken, torn spinach leaves, peanuts, fish sauce, red chilli p213

Chicken & Mint Salad Chicken breasts, Thai mint leaves, chillies, lemon grass p214

Spicy Chicken Salad Carrots, peanuts, chicken, root ginger, fish sauce, lime juice p217

Cucumber Salad Peanuts, red and green chillies, lime peel and juice, dried shrimp, cucumber p219

Prawn Salad with Mint Mildly curried large prawns, tamarind water, Thai mint leaves p220

Squid Salad Beguiling textures of fried squid, lemon grass, Thai mint leaves, cucumber p222

Thai Beef Salad Lean beef, ground browned rice, Thai mint leaves, lime leaves p223

Pork & Bamboo Shoot Salad Finely chopped pork, bamboo shoots, fish sauce, lime juice p225

Chicken & Watercress Finely chopped chicken, roasted peanuts, watercress, peanut oil p226

Hot Bamboo Shoot Salad Warm—and hot—salad of red chilli, bamboo shoots p229

Bean Salad Long beans or green beans, roasted peanuts, Nam Prik, dried red chilli p230

Green Papaya Salad Unripe papaya, dried shrimps, chillies, lime juice, lettuce leaves p232

Fruit Salad Watermelon or honeydew melon, mixed fruits such as lychees, rambutan, kiwifruit p235

Coconut Crêpes Desiccated coconut, coconut milk, caster suger, rice flour p237

Mango with Sticky Rice Coconut milk and cream, ripe mangoes, sticky rice p238

Coconut Custards Melting rounds of eggs, sugar, coconut milk, with rosewater or jasmine essence p240

Green & White Jellies Powdered gelatine, coconut milk and cream, pandanus leaf or kewra water p243

Lychee Sorbet Fresh or tinned lychees, mint leaves, root ginger if desired p244

Lycheees in Coconut Custard Eggs, sugar, coconut milk and cream, lychees p246

Golden Threads Delightful swirls from eggs and sugar, with jasmine essence p246

Thai Sweet-Meats Mung beans, coconut, egg, palm sugar p251

Limeade Limes and sugar, with a surprisingly effective pinch of salt p252

Introduction

Thai food is an original an rich amalgam of evocative aromas, subtle herbs and spices and contrasting textures and tastes. It contains flavours and techniques that are familiar from Chinese, Indian and Japanese cooking, but they have been so skilfully combined and refined that the resulting dishes have a new and exciting character.

The dishes are light and fresh. Vegetables are important, and are quickly cooked to retain their

BELOW: *Fresh fruit often features in Thai meals, carefullly presented for special occasions.*

crispness, flavour and nutrients. Dairy products are not used and fish and poultry feature more prominently than meat; and where this is used it often only constitutes a small portion of the dish.

Equipment is minimal and simple, and the basic preparation of the food and its cooking is straightforward. Thai dishes are cooked quickly, with many taking only a few minutes and the majority no more than 8 to 12 minutes. This factor, coupled with the informal way in which the dishes can be served and eaten, everyone helping themselves, make a Thai meal ideal for today's style of casual entertaining.

Although traditionally all the dishes are served at once, Thai food is so adaptable that there is no problem in dividing it into Western-style courses. Many of the dishes can also be served as snacks or simple one-dish meals.

THE TASTE OF THAI

The flavours that characterise Thai food are the citrus-limes, spiked with clean pine notes, fresh coriander, coconut, garlic and chillies. A fresh sweet-sour taste is also typically Thai, derived from tangy lime or tamarind and palm sugar. Mild fish sauce provides the main savoury flavoring.

Rice is a very important part of the diet. As well as being the foundation of many one-course dishes, rice plays a vital supporting role for other dishes, and dilutes highly spiced ones. A point worth remembering when eating Thai food is that dishes are created specifically to be mixed and eaten with rice.

Thai curries are a case in point, as they can be searingly hot. Unlike Indian curries, Thai curries are cooked quickly and do not have the rich heaviness that results from long, slow simmering. Coconut milk is used to soften the pungency of the spices and combines the contrasting flavours to give a sophisticated subtlety to the finished dish.

Thailand has a long coastline and many inland rivers, which provide fish and shellfish that are both ubiquitous and varied. Freshwater and ocean fish are frequently cooked whole with the head and tail intact, having been cleaned beforehand.

Meat is considered more of a luxury and is often 'stretched' by combining with vegetables, rice, noodles, fish or shellfish, or plenty of coconut-based sauce. Chicken is more abundant, but the birds are smaller than Western farm-reared ones. Duck is popular, particularly for special occasions. Many vegetables are used but they are not often cooked on their own or served as a specific dish. Instead they are combined with meat, poultry or fish and eaten as a salad, either hot or cold, or simply served with 'Nam Prik' (see page 44). The appearance of food matters to the Thais, and they like to add beautifully sculptured garnishes of fruit or vegetables to the finished dishes.

EATING THAI FOOD

Thais eat about 3 cups of rice a day. They might start with a rice soup, perhaps spooned over an egg, or simple fried rice. Lunch will be a composite rice or noodle soup, followed by crisp-fried noodles tossed with a little fish or meat, vegetables or flavorings.

The main meal is eaten in the evening, preferably in the company of an extended family and several friends. Traditionally, Thais will eat sitting on plump cushions set around a low table. All dishes are served simultaneously, rather than as separate courses and everyone shares them.

Surrounding the large central bowl of rice there will be several dishes giving a balanced selection of flavours and textures. Usually they will consist of a soft steamed dish contrasted by a crisp fried one; one that is strongly flavoured (usually 'fired' by chillies), matched by a bland one. There are cool, crunchy salads, bowls of sauces, plus a small bowl of clear soup for each dinner.

There is no structure to the meal. Every diner dips into any dish they choose, putting a portion on their plate to mix with rice. The helpings are always small, but several helpings may be taken from each dish. An ordinary family meal ends with an array of fresh tropical fruits: mangosteens, rambutans, mangoes, papayas, and lychees; all neatly sliced and arranged on special occasions or at formal banquets.

Thais like to eat little and often so throughout the day they will buy ready-made sweets, cakes and savoury snacks from the numerous street vendors. Some of these savoury snacks such as Stuffed Eggs (page 73) and Pork & Noodle Balls (page 79) could be served as a Western-style first course.

COOKING AND EQUIPMENT

Most Thai cooking is done in one piece of cooking equipment, the wok, by either of two very straightforward cooking methods: steaming or stir-frying. Stir-frying is a very rapid process as the ingredients are cut into small, even pieces. For successful stir-frying, heat the wok before adding the oil to help prevent food from sticking, then heat the oil until it is almost smoking before adding the ingredients. Toss the food during cooking and keep it moving from the centre of the wok to the sides. Because of its curved shape, the wok allows the food to be quickly tossed without spilling. As the food is kept moving during stir-frying, very little oil is needed.

Equipment

The amount of equipment needed for Thai cooking is minimal. Moreover, it is possible to prepare and cook Thai food using equipment that is readily at hand in most Western kitchens, but even authentic equipment is now familiar and readily available due to the popularity of Chinese cooking.

Wok—used for frying, stir-frying, deep-frying, and steaming. A useful size to buy is about 30 to 35 cm/

ABOVE: *Western equivalents of Thai equipment can be used perfectly well; but good woks are not expensive.*

12 to 14 inches in diameter. Choose one that has good deep sides and some weight. Carbon steel is preferable to light stainless steel or aluminium as these tend to develop hot spots which cause sticking, and do not withstand intense heat so well. Non-stick and electric woks do not reach sufficiently high temperatures.

A frying pan could be used for frying and stir-frying, a deep-fat fryer for deep frying, and a saucepan for steaming.

Wok-stand—metal ring or stand to hold wok steady over the heat.

Rack—for using in a wok when steaming to support the steaming basket or container of food above the level of the water.

Steamer—Chinese-style bamboo steamers are used in

THAI COOKING: INTRODUCTION

Thailand but Western metal ones will do just as well.

Rice cooker—because of the amount of rice Thais eat and number of people cooked for, many households now use an electric rice cooker. A heavy saucepan with a tight-fitting cover will be adequate for Western needs.

Pestle and mortar—Used during the preparation of the majority of savoury dishes. A small food processor or a coffee grinder kept specifically for the purpose will

ABOVE: *Basic Thai cooking equipment; though today electric rice cookers are even used in Thailand.*

21

ABOVE: *For some tasks, the pestle and mortar are definitely superior to food processors or grinders.*

take away the effort but will not produce quite the same results. When used for fibrous ingredients such as galangal and lemon grass, the pestle and mortar crushes the fibres rather than cuts them and so releases the flavouring juices and oils more successfully.

Knives—Thais use cleavers, but a selection of sizes of good quality sharp knives will suffice.

Spatula—a long handled spatula that is curved and shaped like a shovel for scooping and tossing food in the wok.

Wire baskets—Almost without exception, Thai kitchens have a set of bamboo-handled wire baskets so they can quickly and easily plunge noodles into boiling water for the requisite short cooking time, and then speedily lift them out. Different baskets are used for different types of noodles.

Ingredients

Although some of the foods, principally vegetables, that are available in Thailand cannot easily be found in the West, a sufficiently wide range of ingredients can be obtained to produce authentic Thai dishes. All of the ingredients used in this book can be found without difficulty in oriental and Indian stores, and are becoming increasingly available in good food stores and supermarkets. Suitable alternatives have been mentioned where possible, although they may change the flavour of a recipe.

Banana leaves—used to make containers for steamed foods, to which they impart a delicate taste.

Basil leaves—Thai basil leaves, also called 'holy' basil,

are darker and their flavour slightly deeper, less 'fresh' than ordinary sweet basil. Bundles of leaves can be frozen whole in a plastic bag for up to about 2 weeks; remove leaves as required and add straight to dishes. Substitute Thai sweet basil or ordinary sweet basil, if necessary.

Chillies—add flavour as well as 'heat'. Thais favour small and very fiery 'bird's eye' chillies but these are not available everywhere. Chillies are rarely labelled with an indication of 'hotness', so, as a rule of thumb, smaller varieties are hotter than large ones. Dried chillies have a more earthy, fruity flavor.

The seeds and white veins inside a chilli are not only hotter than the flesh, but have less flavour, and are generally removed before using. Chillies contain an oil

BELOW: *Thai cooks tend to use smaller chillies, those that punch well above their weight in fieriness.*

ABOVE: *Thai sweet basil.*

ABOVE: *Kaffir lime leaves.*

that can make the eyes and even the skin sting, so wash your hands after preparing them and avoid touching your eyes or mouth. To be really safe, wear rubber gloves when handing chillies.

Chinese black mushroom—these dried mushrooms have quite a pronounced flavour and must be soaked for 20 to 30 minutes before use. The stalks tend to be tough so are usually discarded. Available in oriental food stores.

Coconut cream—the layer that forms on top of coconut milk.

Coconut milk—not the liquid from inside a coconut, but extracted from shredded coconut flesh that has been soaked in water. Soak the shredded flesh of 1 medium coconut in 275 ml/10 fl oz of boiling water for 30 minutes. Turn into a strainer lined with muslin or cheesecloth and squeeze the cloth hard to extract as much liquid as possible. Coconut milk can also be made from unsweetened shredded coconut soaked in boiling water, or milk which will be richer. Allow 275 ml/10 fl oz liquid to 450 g/1 lb shredded coconut. Put into a blender and mix for 1 minute. Refrigerate coconut milk.

Ready-prepared coconut milk is sold tinned (which affects the flavour slightly) and in plastic containers.

Coriander leaves—best bought in large bunches rather than small packages. Stand whole bunches in cold water in the refrigerator.

Coriander roots—roots have a more muted taste than the leaves. Large coriander bunches sold in Middle Eastern stores often include the roots. Fresh roots will last for several days if kept wrapped in the refrigerator, or can be frozen. If unavailable, use coriander stalks.

Fish sauce (nam pla)—a clear brown liquid, rich in protein and B vitamins that is the essential Thai seasoning. It is salty but the flavour is mild.

Galangal (galangale, laos, langk haus)—there are

ABOVE: *Coriander.*

Ginger root—When buying fresh ginger root, choose firm, heavy pieces that have a slight sheen. To stow, wrap in paper tissue, place in a plastic bag and store in the vegetable drawer of the refrigerator.

Kaffir limes—slightly smaller than ordinary limes with dark green, knobby peel. The smell and taste of the peel resemble aromatic lime with hints of lemon. The peel of ordinary limes can be substituted. These limes can be difficult to find outside of Thailand.

Kaffir lime leaves—the smooth, dark green leaves give an aromatic, clean citrus-pine flavour and smell. They keep well in a cold place and can be frozen.

Use ordinary lime peel if kaffir lime leaves are unavailable, substituting 1 1/2 teaspoons finely grated peel for 1 kaffir lime leaf.

Lemon grass—a long, slim bulb with a lemon-citrus flavor. To use, cut off the root tip, peel off the tough outer layers and cut away the top part of the stalk. The stalks will keep for several days in the refrigerator, or they can be chopped and frozen. If unavailable, use the grated peel of 1/2 lemon in place of 1 stalk.

two varieties, lesser and greater. The latter is preferred and more likely to be found in the West. It looks similar to ginger root but the skin is thinner, paler, more translucent, and tinged with pink. Its flavour is also similar to ginger but less hot and with definite seductive citrus, pine notes. To use, peel and thickly slice or chop. The whole root will keep for up to 2 weeks if wrapped in paper and kept in the cool drawer of the refrigerator. Or it can be frozen. Allow to defrost just sufficiently to enable the amount required to be sliced off, then return the root to the freezer. Galangal is also sold dried as powder or slices; the latter giving the better flavour. Substitute 1 dried slice or 1 teaspoon powder to each 1.25 cm/1/2 inch used in a recipe; in recipes where fresh galangal is pounded with other spices, mix the dried form in after the pounding; elsewhere, use as normal.

Alternatively, use fresh ginger root.

BELOW: *Apple aubergines and smaller, more bitter pea aubergines are added to Thai curries.*

Long beans—although these can grow to over 3 feet it is best to use younger, smaller ones. Green beans can replace them.

Mint—Thai mint has a spearmint flavour. If not available, use Western spearmint or garden mint.

Noodles—most types are interchangeable but two, rice stick noodles and mung bean noodles, can be crisp-fried. Dried noodles are usually soaked in cold water for 10 to 20 minutes until softened, before cooking; in general, the weight will have doubled after soaking. After draining, the cooking will usually be brief.

BELOW: *Noodle varieties and the popular long-grain white rice known as 'fragrant' rice.*

• Mung bean noodles (glass, shining, bean thread, or cellophane noodles)—tough and semi-transparent raw, they are soaked in warm water before cooking, when they turn to a jelly-like texture.

• Fresh rice noodles—packaged cooked and wet in wide, pliable 'hanks'. To use, without unwinding, cut into ribbons and stir into a dish just to warm through.

• Rice stick noodles (rice vermicelli)—thin, brittle, and semi-transluscent, they are sold in bundles. For most uses the noodles must be soaked before cooking, but when they are to be served crisp they are used dry.

• Egg noodles—these thin wheat flour-based noodles are sold in both fresh (which do not need soaking) and dry 'nests'.

Palm sugar—brown sugar with a slight caramelised flavour. Sold in cakes. If unavailable, substitute 1/2 white and 1/2 demerara sugars.

Pandanus (screwpine)—both the leaves and the distilled essence of the flowers, called kewra water or essence, are used to give an exotic, musky, grassy flavour to sweet dishes.

Pea aubergine—very small aubergines about the size of a pea, and usually the same color, although they can be white, purple, or yellow. The fresh, slightly bitter taste is used raw in hot sauces and cooked in curries. The larger apple aubergines are fairly tasteless but have a pleasing texture and are eaten with Nam Prik.

Rice—Thais mainly use a good quality variety of long-grain white rice called "fragrant" rice. Ordinary long-grain white rice can be substituted. To cook, rinse the rice several times in cold running water. Put the rice into a heavy saucepan with sufficient water according to amount of rice, cover and bring quickly to a boil. Uncover and stir vigorously until the water has evaporated. Reduce the heat to very low, cover the pan tightly with foil, then steam until the rice is tender, light, fluffy, and every grain is separate.

• "Sticky" or "glutinous" rice—an aptly-named short, round grain variety. It can be formed into balls and eaten with fingers, or used for desserts.

• Ground browned rice—sometimes added to dishes to give texture; for this, dry-fry uncooked long-grain white rice until well-browned, then grind finely.

Shallots—Thai red shallots are smaller than Western shallots. They have quite a pronounced flavour that is almost fruity rather than pungent. Ordinary shallots can be substituted.

Shrimp, dried—whole dried shrimp used to add texture and an attractive flavour.

Shrimp paste—a pungent, salty paste that is packed in jars, cans, and plastic packets. It should be kept refrigerated.

Tamarind—sold in sticky brown-black blocks and provides a sharp, slightly fruity taste. To make tamarind water, break off a 25 g/1-ounce piece, pour over 275 ml/10 fl oz boiling water. Break up the lump with a spoon, then leave for about 30 minutes, stirring occasionally. Strain off the tamarind water, pressing on the pulp; discard the remaining debris. Keep the water in a jar in the refrigerator for up to 5 days. Ready-to-use tamarind syrup can sometimes be bought; it is usually more concentrated, so less is used.

NOTE

The nutritional information in this book is intended as a general guideline based on the available information. Salt, fat and sugar content can vary considerably according to the freshness of ingredients and the degree of processing. Always consult your health care professional before making any changes in diet.

Added salt: When a recipe stipulates 'salt to taste' none has been included in the calculation. The amount added will have a dramatic effect on the final sodium content of the dish.

Range of quantities for an ingredient: When the amount of an ingredient is shown as, say 25–50 g, a median value has been used in the calculations.

Calculations per serving: All calculations are per serving or per item, unless otherwise indicated. If it is stated that a recipe 'serves 4–6', then the figures given are for the lower number of people: ie assuming that the meal is shared by four people.

Accompanying sauces: Unless otherwise indicated, accompanying sauces (eg dippiing sauces) have not been included in the nutrient calculation. In any other recipes where the amount of any ingredient is 'to taste' none has been included in the calculation.

GARNISHES

Spring Onion Brushes

[MAKES 4]

4 spring onions

1 Trim away some of the green part of the spring onion. Cut off the white bulb where it starts to turn green.

2 Using a small pair of kitchen scissors, make a cut from the greenest end of the spring onion about halfway along the length. Continue to cut onion into fine strips.

3 Place spring onion into a bowl of chilled water. Leave for a few seconds for strips to curl; lift from water several times to ensure they do not curl too tightly. Repeat with remaining spring onions. Place on absorbent kitchen paper to dry before using.

Chilli Flowers

[MAKES 4]

4 small fresh chillies

1 Cut off top of chilli. Insert scissors in hole and cut through chilli flesh almost to stalk end. Give chilli a quarter turn, make another similar cut then repeat twice more.

2 Remove and discard seeds. Cut through each petal once or twice more to make finer petals.

3 Place in a bowl of chilled water. Leave for 5–10 minutes for the petals to open into a flower shape. Repeat with remaining chillies. Place on absorbent kitchen paper to dry before using.

Banana Leaf Cups

[MAKES 4 CUPS]

**8 pieces banana leaf, each about
12 cm/5 in square**

1 Place 2 pieces of banana leaf with dull sides facing each other. Invert a 10 cm/4 in diameter bowl on top of leaves. Cut around the bowl.

2 Form a 1-cm/$1/2$-in pleat about 4 cm/$1\frac{1}{2}$ in deep in the edge of banana leaf circle. Staple together.

3 Make an identical pleat in the opposite side of circle, then repeat twice more at points equidistant between the 2 pleats, to make a slightly opened, squared-off cup. Repeat with remaining pieces of banana leaf.

Carrot Flowers

[MAKES 6–8]

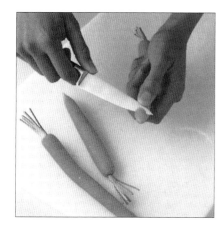

1 young, tender carrot, thinly peeled

1 Hold carrot pointed end down. Using a small, sharp knife make a cut towards the point to form a petal shape. Take care not to slice all the way through. Repeat cuts around carrot to make a flower with 4 petals.

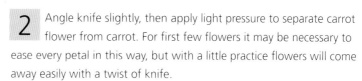

2 Angle knife slightly, then apply light pressure to separate carrot flower from carrot. For first few flowers it may be necessary to ease every petal in this way, but with a little practice flowers will come away easily with a twist of knife.

3 Repeat along length of carrot. Arrange flowers singly or group them into clusters.

NOTE: To improve colour, drop flowers in boiling water, leave for 1 minute then drain and rinse under cold running water. Dry well.

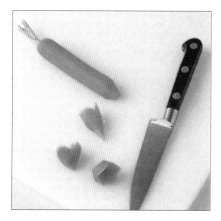

CURRY PASTES, SAUCES & DIPS

Green Curry Paste

[MAKES ABOUT 8 TABLESPOONS]

2 teaspoons coriander seeds
1 teaspoon cumin seeds
1 teaspoon black peppercorns
8 fresh green chillies, seeded
  and chopped
3 shallots, chopped
4 cloves garlic, crushed
3 coriander roots, chopped
2.5-cm/1-in piece galangal,
  chopped
2 stalks lemon grass, chopped
2 kaffir lime leaves, chopped
2 teaspoons shrimp paste
2 tablespoons chopped
  coriander leaves

1 Heat a wok, add the coriander and cumin seeds and heat until the aroma rises.

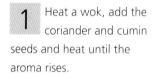

2 Using a pestle and mortar or small blender, crush coriander and cumin seeds with peppercorns.

3 Add remaining ingredients and pound or mix to a smooth paste. Store in an airtight jar in the refrigerator for up to 4 weeks.

NOTE: The yield and hotness will vary according to the size and heat of the chillies.

NUTRITIONAL INFORMATION	
Kcal	80
Protein	8g
Carbs	13g
Fat	4g
Salt	0.6g
Sodium	230mg

Red Curry Paste

[MAKES ABOUT 4 TABLESPOONS]

1 tablespoon coriander seeds
1 teaspoon cumin seeds
1 teaspoon black peppercorns
4 cloves garlic, chopped
3 coriander roots, chopped
8 dried red chillies, seeded and
  chopped
2 stalks lemon grass, chopped
  grated peel $^1/_2$ kaffir lime
3-cm/$1^1/_4$-in piece galangal,
  chopped
2 teaspoons shrimp paste

1 Heat a wok, add coriander and cumin seeds and heat until the aroma rises.

2 Using a pestle and mortar or small blender, crush coriander and cumin seeds with peppercorns.

3 Add remaining ingredients and pound or mix to a smooth paste. Store in an airtight jar in the refrigerator for up to 4 weeks.

NOTE: The yield and hotness will vary according to the size and heat of the chillies.

NUTRITIONAL INFORMATION	
Kcal	30
Protein	7g
Carbs	3g
Fat	4g
Salt	0.6g
Sodium	220mg

37

Fragrant Curry Paste

[MAKES ABOUT 4 TABLESPOONS]

2 cloves garlic, chopped
1 shallot, chopped
4 dried red chillies, seeded and
chopped
1 thick stalk lemon grass, chopped
3 coriander roots, chopped
finely grated peel 2 kaffir limes
1 kaffir lime leaf, torn
4 black peppercorns, cracked
1/2 teaspoon shrimp paste

1 Using a pestle and mortar or small blender, pound or mix together garlic, shallot, chillies, lemon grass and coriander roots.

2 Add lime peel, lime leaf, peppercorns and shrimp paste, and pound or mix to a smooth paste.

3 Store in an airtight jar in the refrigerator for up to 4 weeks.

NUTRITIONAL INFORMATION	
Kcal	30
Protein	2g
Carbs	5g
Fat	Trace
Salt	0.2g
Sodium	60mg

Dipping Sauce 1

[SERVES 4]

8 tablespoons tamarind water, see
    page 27
$1/2$–$3/4$ teaspoon crushed palm
    sugar
1–2 drops fish sauce
$1/2$ teaspoon very finely chopped
    spring onion
$1/2$ teaspoon very finely chopped
    garlic
$1/2$ teaspoon finely chopped fresh
    red chilli

1 In a small saucepan, gently heat tamarind water and sugar until
   sugar has dissolved.

2 Remove pan from heat and add fish sauce. Stir in spring onion,
   garlic and chilli.

3 Pour into a small serving bowl and leave to cool.

NUTRITIONAL INFORMATION	
Kcal	5
Protein	Trace
Carbs	1g
Fat	Trace
Salt	Trace
Sodium	20mg

Dipping Sauce 2

[SERVES 4]

6 tablespoons lime juice
1¹/₂–2 teaspoons crushed palm
  sugar
¹/₂ teaspoon fish sauce
¹/₂ teaspoon very finely chopped
  red shallot
¹/₂ teaspoon very finely chopped
  fresh green chilli
¹/₂ teaspoon finely chopped fresh
  red chilli

1 In a small bowl, stir together lime juice and sugar until sugar has dissolved. Adjust amount of sugar, if desired.

2 Stir in fish sauce, shallot and chillies. Pour into a small serving bowl.

3 Serve with deepfried fish, fish fritters, won tons or spring rolls.

NUTRITIONAL INFORMATION	
Kcal	10
Protein	Trace
Carbs	3g
Fat	Trace
Salt	0.2g
Sodium	60mg

Nam Prik

[SERVES 6–8]

1 tablespoon fish sauce
about 22 whole dried shrimps,
   chopped
3 cloves garlic, chopped
4 dried red chillies with seeds,
   chopped
2 tablespoons lime juice
1 fresh red or green chilli, seeded
   and chopped
about 1 tablespoon pea
   aubergines, if desired, chopped

1 Using a pestle and mortar or small blender, pound or mix fish sauce, shrimps, garlic, dried chillies and lime juice to a paste.

2 Stir in fresh red or green chilli and pea aubergines, if desired. Transfer paste to a small bowl.

3 Serve with a selection of raw vegetables. Store in a covered jar in the refrigerator for several weeks.

NUTRITIONAL INFORMATION	
Kcal	50
Protein	10g
Carbs	1g
Fat	Trace
Salt	2.3g
Sodium	910mg

Spicy Fish Sauce

[SERVES 4]

2 cloves garlic
2 small red or green chillies,
  seeded and chopped
1 tablespoon sugar
2 tablespoons lime juice
2 tablespoons fish sauce

1 Using a pestle and mortar, pound garlic and chillies until finely ground. If you do not have a pestle and mortar, just finely mince the garlic and chillies.

2 Place mixture in a bowl and add sugar, lime juice, fish sauce and 2–3 tablespoons water. Blend well.

3 Spicy Fish Sauce is best served in small dipping saucers.

NOTE: You can make a large quantity of the base for later use by boiling the lime juice, fish sauce and water with sugar in a pan. It will keep for months in a tightly sealed jar in the refrigerator. Add freshly minced garlic and chillies for serving.

NUTRITIONAL INFORMATION	
Kcal	30
Protein	1g
Carbs	7g
Fat	0g
Salt	1.4g
Sodium	560mg

Vegetarian Dipping Sauce

[SERVES 4]

1 tablespoon sugar
2 tablespoons chilli sauce
2–3 tablespoons water
1 small red or green chilli, seeded
  and chopped
1 tablespoon roasted peanuts,
  coarsely chopped

1 In a small bowl, mix the sugar with the chilli sauce and water.

2 Add chopped chilli and transfer the sauce to 4 individual saucers to serve.

3 Sprinkle the chopped peanuts over the top as a garnish.

NOTE: The liquid base can be made in advance; add freshly chopped chilli and the peanuts just before serving.

NUTRITIONAL INFORMATION	
Kcal	40
Protein	1g
Carbs	4g
Fat	2g
Salt	Trace
Sodium	Trace

Roasted Nam Prik

[SERVES 6]

5 fresh red chillies
5 cloves garlic, unpeeled
5 shallots, unpeeled
1 tablespoon shrimp paste (try placing in foil and grilling until darkened)
1 tablespoon tamarind water, see page 27
2 teaspoons crushed palm sugar
2 tablespoons unsalted roasted peanuts

1 Preheat grill. Grill chillies, garlic and shallots, turning occasionally, until skins are an even dark brown. Cool.

2 Peel garlic and shallots, then chop. Chop chillies; do not discard seeds. Using a pestle and mortar or small blender, pound or mix all ingredients to a paste.

3 Serve with cooked vegetables, salads, rice or fish. Store in a covered jar in the refrigerator for up to a week.

NUTRITIONAL INFORMATION	
Kcal	60
Protein	3g
Carbs	6g
Fat	3g
Salt	0.1g
Sodium	50mg

SOUPS &
APPETISERS

Lemon Grass Soup

[SERVES 4]

175–225 g/6–8 oz raw large
prawns
2 teaspoons vegetable oil
625 ml/20 fl oz light fish stock
2 thick stalks lemon grass, finely
chopped
3 tablespoons lime juice
1 tablespoon fish sauce
3 kaffir lime leaves, chopped
1/2 fresh red chilli, seeded and
thinly sliced
1/2 fresh green chilli, seeded and
thinly sliced
1/2 teaspoon crushed palm sugar
coriander leaves, to garnish

1 Peel prawns and remove dark veins running down their backs;
reserve prawn shells.

2 In a wok, heat oil, add prawn shells and fry, stirring occasionally,
until they change colour. Stir in stock, bring to boil and simmer
for 20 minutes. Strain stock and return to wok; discard shells. Add
lemon grass, lime juice, fish sauce, lime leaves, chillies and sugar.
Simmer for 2 minutes.

3 Add prawns and cook just below simmering point for 2–3
minutes until prawns are cooked. Serve in warmed bowls
garnished with coriander.

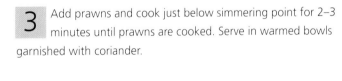

NUTRITIONAL INFORMATION	
Kcal	70
Protein	9g
Carbs	3g
Fat	2g
Salt	1.0g
Sodium	370mg

Vermicelli Soup

[SERVES 4–6]

1.1 litres/2 pints chicken stock
1 small onion, chopped
2 stalks lemon grass, chopped and
  crushed
2 kaffir lime leaves, shredded
1 tablespoon lime juice
3 cloves garlic, chopped
2 fresh red chillies, seeded and
  chopped
4-cm/1½-in piece galangal, peeled
  and chopped

1½ tablespoons fish sauce
2 teaspoons crushed palm sugar
115 g/4 oz clear vermicelli, soaked
  in cold water for 10 minutes,
  drained
2 tablespoons roughly chopped
  coriander leaves
Thai holy basil leaves, to garnish

1 Put stock, onion, lemon grass, lime leaves, lime juice, garlic, chillies and galangal into a saucepan and simmer for 20 minutes.

2 Stir in fish sauce and sugar. When sugar has dissolved, add noodles and cook for 1 minute.

3 Stir in coriander. Spoon into warmed bowls and garnish with basil leaves.

NUTRITIONAL INFORMATION	
Kcal	140
Protein	4g
Carbs	31g
Fat	Trace
Salt	1.1g
Sodium	450mg

Chicken & Mushroom Soup

[SERVES 4]

2 cloves garlic, crushed
4 coriander sprigs
1¹/₂ teaspoons black peppercorns, crushed
1 tablespoon vegetable oil
1 litre/35 fl oz chicken stock
5 pieces dried Chinese black mushrooms, soaked in cold water for 20 minutes, drained and coarsely chopped

1 tablespoon fish sauce
115 g/4 oz chicken, cut into strips
55 g/2 oz spring onions, thinly sliced
coriander sprigs, to garnish

1 Using a pestle and mortar or small blender, pound or mix garlic, coriander stalks and leaves and peppercorns to a paste. In a wok, heat oil, add paste and cook, stirring, for 1 minute.

2 Stir in stock, mushrooms and fish sauce. Simmer for 5 minutes.

3 Add chicken, lower heat so liquid barely moves and cook gently for 5 minutes. Scatter spring onions over surface and garnish with coriander sprigs.

NUTRITIONAL INFORMATION	
Kcal	80
Protein	7g
Carbs	2g
Fat	5g
Salt	0.8g
Sodium	310mg

Pork & Peanut Soup

[SERVES 3–4]

4 coriander roots, chopped
2 cloves garlic, chopped
1 teaspoon black peppercorns, cracked
1 tablespoon vegetable oil
225 g/8 oz lean pork, finely chopped
4 spring onions, chopped

700 ml/24 fl oz veal stock
55 g/2 oz skinned peanuts
6 pieces dried Chinese black mushrooms, soaked for 20 minutes, drained and chopped
115 g/4 oz bamboo shoots, roughly chopped
1 tablespoon fish sauce

1 Using a pestle and mortar, pound coriander, garlic and peppercorns to a paste.

2 In a wok, heat oil, add peppercorn paste and cook for 2–3 minutes, stirring occasionally. Add pork and spring onions and stir for 1^1/$_2$ minutes.

3 Stir stock, peanuts and mushrooms into wok, then cook at just below boiling point for 7 minutes. Add bamboo. shoots and fish sauce and continue to cook gently for 3–4 minutes.

NUTRITIONAL INFORMATION	
Kcal	270
Protein	21g
Carbs	3g
Fat	19g
Salt	0.1g
Sodium	60mg

Chicken & Coconut Soup

[SERVES 4]

950 ml/30 fl oz coconut milk
115 g/4 oz chicken breast meat,
   cut into strips
2 stalks lemon grass, bruised and
   thickly sliced
2 spring onions, thinly sliced
3–4 fresh red chillies, seeded and
   sliced

juice 1½ limes
1 tablespoon fish sauce
1 tablespoon coriander leaves,
   freshly torn into shreds
coriander leaves, to garnish

1 Bring coconut milk to just below boiling point in a saucepan. Add chicken and lemon grass.

2 Adjust heat so liquid gives just an occasional bubble, then poach chicken, uncovered, for about 4 minutes until tender.

3 Add spring onions and chillies. Heat briefly, then remove from heat and stir in lime juice, fish sauce and shredded coriander. Serve garnished with coriander leaves.

NUTRITIONAL INFORMATION	
Kcal	420
Protein	12g
Carbs	7g
Fat	39g
Salt	0.8g
Sodium	310mg

Seafood Soup

[SERVES 4–6]

1 tablespoon vegetable oil
1/2 teaspoon minced garlic
2 small fresh red chillies, seeded
  and chopped
1 tablespoon chopped onion
685 m/(24 fl oz chicken stock
225 g/8 oz squid, prepared as for
  Squid with Chillies, page 133
115 g/4 oz fresh scallops, sliced
115 g/4 oz raw peeled prawns

2–3 tablespoons lime juice or
  vinegar
1 tablespoon sugar
3 tablespoons fish sauce
225 g/8 oz bean sprouts
1/4 cucumber, thinly shredded
salt and freshly ground black
  pepper
coriander sprigs, to garnish

1 Heat the oil in a wok or pan and lightly brown garlic, chillies and onion. Add stock and bring to a rolling boil. Stir in the squid, scallops, prawns, lime juice or vinegar, sugar and fish sauce. Simmer for 2 minutes.

2 Add bean sprouts and shredded cucumber, bring back to boil and adjust the seasoning.

3 Serve the soup piping hot, garnished with coriander sprigs.

NOTE: The seafood and vegetables must not be overcooked, or the seafood will be tough and the vegetables lose their crispiness.

NUTRITIONAL INFORMATION	
Kcal	180
Protein	23g
Carbs	11g
Fat	5g
Salt	2.7g
Sodium	1080mg

Papaya & Pork Soup

[SERVES 4]

1 litre/35 fl oz stock or water
4 pork chops, each weighing
   about 85 g/3 oz
1 small unripe green papaya,
   peeled and cut into small cubes
2 tablespoons fish sauce
salt and freshly ground black
   pepper
1 tablespoon chopped spring
   onions
coriander sprigs, to garnish

1 Bring stock or water to the boil in a wok or pan and add the pork. Bring back to boil and skim off the scum, then reduce heat, cover and simmer gently for 25–30 minutes.

2 Add the papaya cubes and fish sauce, bring back to boil and cook the soup for a further 5 minutes.

3 To serve, place salt, pepper and the chopped spring onions in a tureen. Pour the boiling soup with its content over it, garnish with coriander sprigs and serve at once. The meat should be so tender that one can easily tear it apart into small pieces for eating.

NUTRITIONAL INFORMATION	
Kcal	320
Protein	14g
Carbs	9g
Fat	25g
Salt	1.6g
Sodium	630mg

Gold Bags

[MAKES 16]

115 g/4 oz cooked peeled prawns,
  finely chopped
55 g/2 oz tinned water chestnuts,
  finely chopped
2 spring onions, white part only,
  finely chopped
1 teaspoon fish sauce
freshly ground black pepper
16 won ton skins
vegetable oil for deep frying
Dipping Sauce 1, see page 41
coriander sprig, to garnish

1 In a bowl, mix together prawns, water chestnuts, spring onions , fish sauce and black pepper.

2 To shape each bag, put a small amount of prawn mixture in centre of each won ton skin. Dampen edges of skins with a little water, then bring up over filling to form a 'dolly bag'. Press edges together to seal.

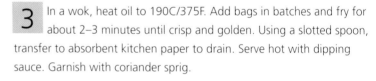

3 In a wok, heat oil to 190C/375F. Add bags in batches and fry for about 2–3 minutes until crisp and golden. Using a slotted spoon, transfer to absorbent kitchen paper to drain. Serve hot with dipping sauce. Garnish with coriander sprig.

NUTRITIONAL INFORMATION	
Kcal	200
Protein	8g
Carbs	11g
Fat	14g
Salt	1.4g
Sodium	550mg

Corn Cakes

[MAKES 16]

350 g/12 oz sweetcorn kernels
1 tablespoon Green Curry Paste,
   see page 35
2 tablespoons plain flour
3 tablespoons rice flour
3 spring onions, finely chopped
1 egg, beaten
2 teaspoons fish sauce
vegetable oil for deep frying
2.5-cm/1-in piece cucumber
Dipping Sauce 2, see page 43
1 tablespoon ground roasted
   peanuts

1 Place sweetcorn in a blender, add curry paste, plain flour, rice flour, spring onions, egg and fish sauce and mix together so corn is slightly broken up. Form into about 16 cakes.

2 Heat oil in a wok to 175C/350F, then deep fry one batch of sweetcorn cakes for about 3 minutes until golden brown. Using a slotted spoon, transfer to absorbent kitchen paper to drain. Keep warm while frying remaining cakes.

3 Peel cucumber, quarter lengthways, remove seeds, then slice thinly. Place in a small bowl and mix in dipping sauce and ground peanuts. Serve with warm corn cakes.

NUTRITIONAL INFORMATION	
Kcal (Whole recipe)	350
Protein	7g
Carbs	40g
Fat	18g
Salt	1.3g
Sodium	500mg

Stuffed Chicken Wings

[SERVES 4]

4 large chicken wings
lean pork, finely minced, (see
    method)
55 g/2 oz cooked peeled prawns,
    chopped
3 spring onions, finely chopped
2 large cloves garlic, chopped

3 coriander roots, chopped
2 tablespoons fish sauce
freshly ground black pepper
vegetable oil for deep frying
rice flour for coating
Dipping Sauce 2, see page 43
lettuce leaves, to garnish

1   Bend wing joints backwards against joint. Using a small sharp knife or kitchen scissors, cut around top of bone that attaches wing to chicken body. Using blade of knife, scrape meat and skin down length of first bone, turning skin back over unboned portion. Break bone free at joint.Ease skin over joint and detach from flesh and bone.

2   Working down next adjacent bones, scrape off flesh and skin taking care not to puncture skin. Break bones free at joint, leaving end section. Chop chicken flesh from wings. Make up to 175 g/ 6 oz with pork, if necessary. Place chicken and pork, if used, in a bowl and thoroughly mix together with prawns and spring onions.

3   Divide between chicken wings; set aside. Using a pestle and mortar, pound together garlic and coriander roots. Stir in fish sauce and plenty of black pepper. Pour over chicken wings, stirring them to coat with mixture. Set aside for 30 minutes. Heat oil in a wok to 180C/ 350F. Remove chicken wings from bowl, then toss in rice flour to coat completely. Add 2 at a time to oil and deep fry for about 3–4 minutes until browned. Using a slotted spoon, transfer to absorbent kitchen paper to drain. Serve with sauce and garnish with lettuce leaves.

NUTRITIONAL INFORMATION	
Kcal	210
Protein	17g
Carbs	7g
Fat	13g
Salt	1.6g
Sodium	630mg

Steamed Eggs

[SERVES 2–4]

6 eggs, beaten
2 spring onions, thinly sliced
85 g/3 oz cooked peeled
   prawns, finely chopped
freshly ground black pepper
1 fresh red chilli, seeded and
   thinly sliced
1 tablespoon chopped coriander
   leaves
75 ml/2½ fl oz coconut milk
2 teaspoons fish sauce
coriander sprigs and red chilli
   rings, to garnish

1 In a small blender or food processor, mix all ingredients except coriander sprigs until evenly combined.

2 Pour into greased individual heatproof dishes. Place in a steaming basket, then position over a saucepan of boiling water. Cover and steam for 10–12 minutes until just set in centre.

3 Remove from heat, leave to stand for a minute or two. Turn out onto a plate, then invert onto a warmed plate. Garnish with coriander sprigs and red chilli rings.

NUTRITIONAL INFORMATION	
Kcal	300
Protein	27g
Carbs	3g
Fat	20g
Salt	3.1g
Sodium	1230mg

Stuffed Eggs

[SERVES 4]

4 large eggs, at room
  temperature
4 tablespoons minced cooked
  pork
4 tablespoons finely chopped
  peeled prawns
1 teaspoon fish sauce
1 clove garlic, finely chopped
1½ tablespoons chopped
  coriander leaves
finely ground black pepper
lettuce leaves, to serve
coriander sprigs, to garnish

1 Form 4 nests from foil to hold eggs upright. Place in a steaming basket. Cook eggs in pan of gently boiling water for 1½ minutes; remove.

2 Carefully peel a small part of pointed end of eggs. With the point of a slim, sharp knife, cut a small hole down through the exposed white of each egg; reserve pieces of white that are removed. Pour liquid egg yolk and white from egg into a small bowl. Thoroughly mix in pork, prawns, fish sauce, garlic, coriander and pepper. Carefully spoon into eggs and replace removed pieces of white.

3 Set steaming basket over a saucepan of boiling water and place eggs, cut end uppermost, in foil nests. Cover basket and steam eggs for about 12 minutes. When cool enough to handle, carefully peel off shells. Serve whole or halved on lettuce leaves, garnished with coriander sprigs.

NUTRITIONAL INFORMATION	
Kcal	150
Protein	14g
Carbs	Trace
Fat	10g
Salt	1.1g
Sodium	430mg

Egg Nests
[SERVES 4]

1 tablespoon chopped coriander
  roots
1 clove garlic, chopped
1/2 teaspoon black peppercorns,
  cracked
1 tablespoon peanut oil
1/2 small onion, finely chopped
115 g/4 oz lean pork, very finely
  chopped

115 g/4 oz raw peeled prawns,
  chopped
2 teaspoons fish sauce
3 tablespoons vegetable oil
2 eggs
3 fresh red chillies, seeded and cut
  into fine strips
20–30 coriander leaves
coriander sprigs, to garnish

1 Using a pestle and mortar, pound together coriander roots, garlic and peppercorns. In a wok, heat peanut oil, add peppercorn mixture and onion and stir-fry for 1 minute. Add pork, stir-fry for 1 minute, then stir in prawns for 45 seconds. Quickly stir in fish sauce, then transfer mixture to a bowl. Using kitchen paper, wipe out wok.

2 Add vegetable oil to wok and place over medium heat. In a bowl, beat eggs. Spoon egg into a cone of greaseproof paper with a very small hole in pointed end. Move cone above surface of pan, so trail of egg flows onto it and sets in threads. Quickly repeat in another direction over threads. Repeat until there are 4 crisscrossing layers.

3 Using a spatula, transfer nest to absorbent kitchen paper. Repeat with remaining egg to make more nests. Place nests with flat side facing downwards. Place 2 strips of chilli to form a cross on each nest. Top with coriander leaves, then about 1 tablespoon of pork mixture. Fold nests over filling, turn over and arrange on serving plate. Garnish with coriander sprigs.

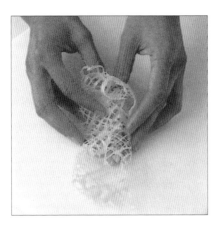

NUTRITIONAL INFORMATION	
Kcal	240
Protein	15g
Carbs	3g
Fat	18g
Salt	0.8g
Sodium	310mg

Son-in-Law Eggs

[SERVES 6]

vegetable oil for deep frying
6 eggs, hard-boiled and shelled
1 small onion, thinly sliced
2 tablespoons fish sauce
2 teaspoons crushed palm sugar
1 fresh red chilli, seeded and cut
   into fine slivers
Chilli Flowers, see page 30, to
   garnish

1 Heat oil in a wok, add eggs and cook, turning occasionally, until golden. Using a slotted spoon, transfer to absorbent kitchen paper to drain, then halve lengtways. Place, cut side uppemost, on serving plates; set aside.

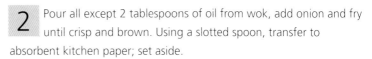

2 Pour all except 2 tablespoons of oil from wok, add onion and fry until crisp and brown. Using a slotted spoon, transfer to absorbent kitchen paper; set aside.

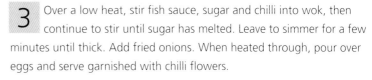

3 Over a low heat, stir fish sauce, sugar and chilli into wok, then continue to stir until sugar has melted. Leave to simmer for a few minutes until thick. Add fried onions. When heated through, pour over eggs and serve garnished with chilli flowers.

NUTRITIONAL INFORMATION	
Kcal	170
Protein	8g
Carbs	6g
Fat	13g
Salt	1.2g
Sodium	460mg

Pork & Noodle Balls

[MAKES ABOUT 12 PARCELS]

3 cloves garlic, chopped
4 coriander roots, chopped
175 g/6 oz lean pork, minced
1 small egg, beaten
2 teaspoons fish sauce
freshly ground black pepper
about 55 g/2 oz egg thread
 noodles (1 nest)
vegetable oil for deep frying
Dipping Sauce 1, see page 41, to
 serve
coriander sprig, to garnish

1 Using a pestle and mortar or small blender, pound or mix together garlic and coriander roots. In a bowl, mix together pork, egg, fish sauce and pepper, then stir in garlic mixture.

2 Place noodles in a heatproof sieve and dip in boiling water for 5 seconds if fresh, about 2 minutes if dried, until separated. Remove and rinse immediately in cold running water. Form pork mixture into approximately 12 balls. Neatly and evenly wind 3 or 4 strands of noodles around each ball to cover completely.

3 In a wok, heat oil to 180C/350F. Lower 4–6 balls into oil and cook for about 3 minutes until golden and pork is cooked through. Using a slotted spoon, transfer to kitchen paper to drain. Keep warm while cooking others. Serve hot with dipping sauce.

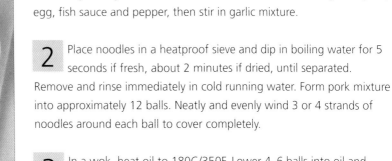

NUTRITIONAL INFORMATION	
Kcal	70
Protein	4g
Carbs	3g
Fat	5g
Salt	0.3g
Sodium	120mg

Pork Toasts

[SERVES 4–6]

175 g/6 oz lean pork, minced
55 g/2 oz cooked peeled prawns, finely chopped
2 cloves garlic, finely chopped
1 tablespoon chopped coriander leaves
1½ spring onions, finely chopped
2 eggs, beaten

2 teaspoons fish sauce
freshly ground black pepper
4 day-old slices of bread
1 tablespoon coconut milk
vegetable oil for deep frying
coriander leaves, fine rings of fresh red chilli and cucumber slices, to garnish

1 In a bowl, mix together pork and prawns using a fork, then thoroughly mix in garlic, coriander, spring onions, half of egg, the fish sauce and black pepper. Divide between bread, spreading it firmly to edges.

2 In a small bowl, stir together remaining egg and coconut milk and brush over pork mixture. Trim crusts from bread, then cut each slice into squares. In a wok, heat oil to 190C/375F.

3 Add several squares at a time, pork-side down, and fry for 3–4 minutes until crisp, turning over halfway through. Using a slotted spoon, transfer to absorbent kitchen paper to drain, then keep warm in oven. Check temperature of oil in between frying each batch. Serve warm, garnished with coriander and slices of chilli and cucumber.

NUTRITIONAL INFORMATION	
Kcal	310
Protein	19g
Carbs	19g
Fat	18g
Salt	1.7g
Sodium	680mg

Sesame Prawn Toasts

[SERVES 6–8]

225–300 g/8–10 oz raw peeled
  prawns, chopped
1/2 teaspoon minced garlic
1/2 teaspoon finely chopped
  fresh root ginger
2 shallots or 1 small onion,
  finely chopped
1 egg, beaten
salt and freshly ground black
  pepper
1 tablespoon cornflour
1 French baguette
3–4 tablespoons white sesame
  seeds
oil for deep-frying
chopped fresh coriander leaves,
  to garnish

1   In a bowl, mix the prawns, garlic, ginger, shallots, egg, salt, pepper and cornflour and chill in the refrigerator for at least 2 hours.

2   Cut the bread into 1 cm/1/2 in slices and spread thickly with prawn mixture on one side, then press that side down onto the sesame seeds so that the entire surface is covered by the seeds, making sure the seeds are firmly pressed into the prawn mixture.

3   Heat the oil in a wok or deep-fat fryer to 180C/350F and deep-fry the toasts, in batches, spread-side down, for 2–3 minutes until they start to turn golden brown around the edges. Remove and drain on absorbent kitchen paper. Serve hot, garnished with chopped coriander leaves.

NUTRITIONAL INFORMATION	
Kcal	420
Protein	17g
Carbs	41g
Fat	22g
Salt	1.2g
Sodium	480mg

Steamed Tofu & Fish Sauce

[SERVES 4]

1 tablespoon dried shrimp
55 g/2 oz minced pork
2 tablespoons chopped
   preserved vegetable, eg mildly
   pickled
1 tablespoon chopped spring
   onions
salt and freshly ground black
   pepper, to taste
1 teaspoon sesame oil
1 tablespoon vegetable oil
2 cakes tofu, each cut into 4
   squares
2 tablespoons fish sauce
coriander sprigs, to garnish

1 In a bowl, mix the shrimp, pork, preserved vegetable, spring onions, salt, pepper and sesame oil. Blend well and set aside.

2 Grease a heatproof plate with the vegetable oil and place the tofu on it. Pour the fish sauce evenly all over the tofu, then place about 1 tablespoon of the shrimp and pork mixture on top of each square.

3 Place the plate with the tofu in a hot steamer, cover and cook over high heat for 12–15 minutes. Serve at once, garnished with coriander sprigs.

NUTRITIONAL INFORMATION	
Kcal	130
Protein	10g
Carbs	3g
Fat	8g
Salt	1.5g
Sodium	580mg

Stuffed Omelette

[SERVES 4–6]

2¹/₂ tablespoons vegetable oil
1 small onion, quartered and
  thinly sliced
3 cloves garlic, chopped
8 coriander roots, chopped
14 black peppercorns, cracked
150 g/5 oz lean pork, very finely
  chopped

150 g/5 oz long beans, or green
  beans, thinly sliced and cut into
  3-cm/1¹/₄-in lengths
8 eggs, beaten
2 teaspoons fish sauce
4 tablespoons chopped coriander
  leaves
coriander sprigs, to garnish

1 In a wok, heat 2 tablespoons oil, add onion and cook, stirring until lightly browned.

2 Using a pestle and mortar or small blender, pound or mix together garlic, coriander roots and peppercorns. Stir into wok and cook, stirring occasionally, for 2 minutes. Add pork, stir-fry for 2 minutes, then stir in beans. Stir-fry for 2 minutes. Cover wok and set aside.

3 In a small bowl, mix eggs with fish sauce and coriander. In a frying pan, heat remaining oil, pour in half of egg mixture and tilt pan to form a thin, even layer. Cook briefly until lightly set. Spoon half of reserved filling down the centre. Fold sides over filling to form a square package, then slide onto a warmed plate. Keep warm while making second omelette with remaining egg and filling. Garnish with coriander sprigs.

NUTRITIONAL INFORMATION	
Kcal	330
Protein	25g
Carbs	5g
Fat	24g
Salt	1.0g
Sodium	390mg

Steamed Crab

[SERVES 4]

1 clove garlic, chopped
1 small shallot, chopped
6 coriander sprigs, stalks finely
   chopped
175 g/6 oz cooked crab meat
115 g/4 oz lean pork, very finely
   chopped and cooked
1 egg, beaten
1 tablespoon coconut cream, see
   page 24
2 teaspoons fish sauce
freshly ground black pepper
1 fresh red chilli, seeded and cut
   into fine strips

1 Grease 4 individual heatproof dishes and place in a steaming basket.

2 Using a pestle and mortar, pound garlic, shallot and coriander stalks to a paste. In a bowl, stir together crab meat, pork, garlic paste, egg, coconut cream, fish sauce and plenty of black pepper until evenly mixed.

3 Divide between dishes, arrange coriander leaves and strip of chilli on tops. Place steaming basket over a saucepan of boiling water and steam for about 12 minutes until mixture is firm.

NOTE: Crab shells may be used instead of dishes for cooking.

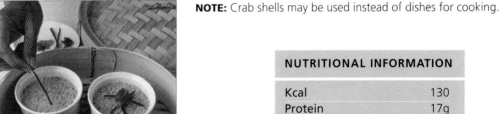

NUTRITIONAL INFORMATION	
Kcal	130
Protein	17g
Carbs	2g
Fat	7g
Salt	1.0g
Sodium	390mg

Stuffed Courgettes

[SERVES 4–6]

55 g/2 oz fresh coconut, grated
6 tablespoons chopped coriander
  leaves
1 fresh green chilli, seeded and
  finely chopped
4 courgettes, about 225 g/8 oz
  each

5 tablespoons vegetable oil
few drops fish sauce
2 tablespoons lime juice
1 teaspoon crushed palm sugar
freshly ground black pepper

1 In a small bowl, combine coconut, coriander and chilli; set aside. Cut each courgette into 4 lengths, about 4 cm/1$\frac{1}{2}$ in long. Stand each on one cut side and cut 2 deep slits like a cross, down 2.5 cm (1 in) of the length.

2 Gently prise apart cut sections and fill with coconut mixture. Pour oil and 125 ml/4 fl oz water into a wide frying pan. Stand courgettes, filled side uppermost, in pan. Sprinkle over a little fish sauce. If any coconut mixture remains, spoon over courgettes.

3 Sprinkle over lime juice, sugar, black pepper and a few drops of fish sauce. Heat to simmering point, cover tightly and simmer gently for 5–6 minutes. Using 2 spoons, turn courgette pieces over, re-cover and cook for a further 7-10 minutes so some bite is retained.

NUTRITIONAL INFORMATION	
Kcal	240
Protein	5g
Carbs	6g
Fat	22g
Salt	Trace
Sodium	Trace

Crab Rolls

[MAKES ABOUT 36]

225 g/8 oz cooked chicken, very finely chopped
115 g/4 oz cooked crabmeat, flaked
4 spring onions, finely chopped
25 g/1 oz beansprouts, finely chopped
1 small carrot, grated
2 teaspoons fish sauce

freshly ground black pepper
about 9 rice paper wrappers, each about 18 cm/7 in in diameter
vegetable oil for deep frying
Thai holy basil leaves, Thai mint leaves and lettuce leaves, to serve
Dipping Sauce 1, see page 41

1 In a bowl, mix together chicken, crabmeat, spring onions, beansprouts, carrot, fish sauce and black pepper. Brush both sides of each wrapper liberally with water and set aside to soften.

2 Cut each into wedges. Place a small amount of filling near wide end of one wedge, fold end over filling, tuck in sides and roll up. Repeat with remaining wedges and filling.

3 In a wok, heat oil to 190C/375F. Fry rolls in batches for 2–3 minutes until crisp and golden. Drain on absorbent kitchen paper. Serve hot. To eat, sprinkle each roll with herbs, then wrap in a lettuce leaf and dip into dipping sauce.

NUTRITIONAL INFORMATION	
Kcal (For 6)	230
Protein	14g
Carbs	2g
Fat	18g
Salt	0.6g
Sodium	230mg

FISH & SHELLFISH

Steamed Fish

[SERVES 4]

1 whole fish, such as sea bass,
  grey mullet or grouper,
  weighing about 900 g/2 lb,
  cleaned and scored on both
  sides at 2.5-cm/1-in intervals
salt and freshly ground black
  pepper, to taste
1 teaspoon sugar
1 teaspoon chopped fresh root
  ginger
1 tablespoon each chopped
  white and green parts of
  spring onions
1 tablespoon fish sauce
2 teaspoons sesame oil
1 tablespoon shredded fresh
  root ginger
1 tablespoon vegetable oil
1 tablespoon each black bean
  sauce and soy sauce
2 small fresh red chillies, seeded
  and shredded coriander sprigs,
  to garnish

1 Rub the fish inside and out with salt and pepper, then marinate in a shallow dish with the sugar, ginger, white parts of spring onions, the fish sauce and sesame oil for 30 minutes. Place fish with marinade in a hot steamer, or on a rack inside a wok, cover and steam for 15–20 minutes. Remove dish from the steamer or wok.

2 Put ginger and green onion pieces on top of fish. Heat vegetable oil in a small saucepan and add black bean sauce.

3 Add soy sauce and chillies and stir-fry for 30 seconds, then drizzle it over fish. Garnish with coriander and serve with rice and a salad.

NUTRITIONAL INFORMATION

Kcal	160
Protein	23g
Carbs	3g
Fat	6g
Salt	1.1g
Sodium	420mg

Fried Fish Fillet

[SERVES 4]

450 g/1 lb firm white fish fillet,
  such as halibut, cod, haddock or
  monkfish, cut into 2-cm/³/4-in
  pieces
salt and freshly ground black
  pepper, to taste
1 egg, beaten
3 tablespoons plain flour mixed
  with 2 tablespoons water
vegetable oil for deep-frying
fresh holy basil and coriander
  sprigs, to garnish
Spicy Fish Sauce, page 47, to serve

1 In a dish, season the fish with salt and pepper and leave for 25–30 minutes. Make a batter by blending the beaten egg with the flour and water paste.

2 Heat oil in a wok or deep-fat fryer to 180C/350F. Coat the fish pieces with batter and deep-fry them, in batches, for 3–4 minutes until golden. Remove and drain.

3 Place the fish pieces on a warmed serving dish with the garnishes. Serve at once with the Spicy Fish Sauce as a dip.

VARIATION: A whole fish, boned, skinned and coated in batter, can be deep-fried first then cut into bite-sized pieces for serving.

NUTRITIONAL INFORMATION	
Kcal	240
Protein	23g
Carbs	9g
Fat	13g
Salt	0.3g
Sodium	110mg

Fish with Galangal

[SERVES 3–4]

2 fresh red chillies, seeded and
   finely chopped
2 cloves garlic, finely chopped
1 shallot, finely chopped
4-cm/1¹/₂-in piece galangal, finely
   chopped
2 stalks lemon grass, finely
   chopped

1 tablespoon fish sauce
20 Thai holy basil leaves
450 g/1 lb boneless firm white
   fish, such as halibut, cod, hake or
   monkfish, cut into about 2-cm/
   ³/₄-in pieces
banana leaves, if desired

1 Using a pestle and mortar or small blender, briefly mix together chillies, garlic, shallot, galangal, lemon grass and fish sauce. Turn into a bowl, stir in basil leaves and fish.

2 Divide between 3 or 4 pieces banana leaf or foil. Fold leaves or foil over fish to make neat parcels. Secure leaves with a wooden cocktail stick, or fold foil edges tightly together.

3 Put parcels in a steaming basket. Place over boiling water and steam for about 7 minutes until fish is lightly cooked.

NUTRITIONAL INFORMATION	
Kcal	130
Protein	27g
Carbs	3g
Fat	1g
Salt	1.2g
Sodium	490mg

Fish with Lemon Grass

[SERVES 2]

2 tablespoons vegetable oil
1 flat fish, such as pomfret, plump lemon sole or plaice, gutted and cleaned
4 cloves garlic, finely chopped
2 fresh red chillies, seeded and finely chopped
1 red shallot, chopped

4^1/$_2$ tablespoons lime juice
^{1}/$_2$ teaspoon crushed palm sugar
1^1/$_2$ tablespoons finely chopped lemon grass
2 teaspoons fish sauce
Chilli Flowers, see page 30, to garnish

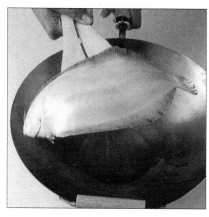

1 In a wok, heat oil, add fish, skin-side down first, and cook for 3–5 minutes a side until lightly browned and lightly cooked.

2 Using a fish slice, transfer to a warmed serving plate, cover and keep warm. Add garlic to wok and fry, stirring occasionally, until browned.

3 Stir in chillies, shallot, lime juice, sugar, lemon grass and fish sauce. Allow to simmer gently for 1–2 minutes. Pour over fish and garnish with chilli flowers.

NUTRITIONAL INFORMATION	
Kcal	320
Protein	36g
Carbs	4g
Fat	17g
Salt	1.6g
Sodium	620mg

Fish with Coriander & Garlic

[SERVES 2]

6 coriander roots, chopped
3 large cloves garlic, chopped
5 black peppercorns, crushed
2 fish fillets, such as trout or plaice
2 pieces banana leaf, if desired
3 tablespoons lime juice
1/2 teaspoon crushed palm sugar

1 spring onion, finely chopped
1/2 small fresh green chilli, seeded
  and thinly sliced
1/2 small fresh red chilli, seeded
  and thinly sliced
Chilli Flowers, see page 30, to
  garnish

1 Using a pestle and mortar or small blender, briefly mix together coriander roots, garlic and peppercorns. Spread evenly over inside of fish fillets; set aside for 30 minutes.

2 Wrap fish in banana leaves or pieces of foil, securing leaf with wooden cocktail stick, or folding edges of foil tightly together. Grill for about 8 minutes.

3 Meanwhile, in a bowl, stir together lime juice and sugar, then stir in spring onion and chillies. Serve with fish. Garnish with chilli flowers.

NUTRITIONAL INFORMATION	
Kcal	100
Protein	18g
Carbs	2g
Fat	2g
Salt	0.3g
Sodium	120mg

Fish with Mushroom Sauce

[SERVES 2]

plain flour
salt and freshly ground black
    pepper, to taste
1 whole flat fish, such as pomfret,
    plump lemon sole or plaice,
    about 700 g/1¹/₂ lb, gutted and
    cleaned
2 tablespoons vegetable oil plus
    extra for deep frying
3 cloves garlic, thinly sliced

1 small onion, halved and thinly
    sliced
4.5-cm/1³/₄-in piece fresh root
    ginger, finely chopped
115 g/4 oz shiitake mushrooms,
    sliced
2 teaspoons fish sauce
3 spring onions, sliced
Spring Onion Brushes, see page
    29, to garnish

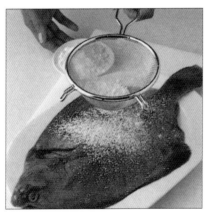

1 Season flour with salt and pepper, then use to lightly dust fish. Heat oil in a large deep fat frying pan to 180C/350F, add fish and cook for 4–5 minutes, turning halfway through, until crisp and browned.

2 Meanwhile, heat 2 tablespoons oil in a wok, add garlic, onion and ginger and cook, stirring occasionally, for 2 minutes. Add mushrooms and stir-fry for 2 minutes. Stir in fish sauce, 3–4 tablespoons water and spring onions. Bubble briefly.

3 Using a fish slice, transfer fish to absorbent kitchen paper to drain. Put on a warmed serving plate and spoon over sauce. Garnish with spring onion brushes.

NUTRITIONAL INFORMATION	
Kcal	430
Protein	34g
Carbs	15g
Fat	27g
Salt	1.5g
Sodium	580mg

Fish in Coconut Sauce

[SERVES 3–4]

4 tablespoons vegetable oil
1 shallot, chopped
4-cm/1¹/₂-in piece galangal, finely
   chopped
2 stalks lemon grass, finely
   chopped
1 small fresh red chilli, seeded and
   chopped

125 ml/4 fl oz coconut milk
2 teaspoons fish sauce
5 coriander sprigs
about 350 g/12 oz white fish
   fillets, such as halibut, red
   snapper
1 small onion, sliced
freshly ground black pepper

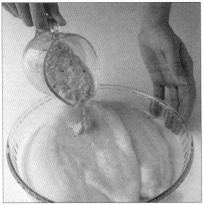

1 In a wok, heat 1 tablespoon oil, add shallot, galangal, lemon grass and chilli. Stir for a few minutes until lightly coloured. Transfer to a small blender, add coconut milk, fish sauce and stalks from coriander sprigs and process until well mixed.

2 Place fish in a heatproof, shallow round dish that fits over a saucepan, and pour over spice sauce. Cover dish, place over pan of boiling water and steam for minutes until flesh flakes.

3 Meanwhile, heat remaining oil in a wok over moderate heat, add onion and cook, stirring occasionally, until browned. Using a slotted spoon, transfer to kitchen paper. Add coriander leaves to oil and fry for a few seconds. Using a slotted spoon, transfer to kitchen paper to drain. Scatter fried onions and coriander over fish and add pepper.

NUTRITIONAL INFORMATION	
Kcal	330
Protein	22g
Carbs	6g
Fat	25g
Salt	0.9g
Sodium	340mg

Fish with Tamarind & Ginger

[SERVES 4]

6 tablespoons vegetable oil
1 kg/2^{1}/$_{2}$ lb whole white fish or
  single piece, such as cod, bass or
  red snapper
1 small onion, finely chopped
6 spring onions, thickly sliced
2 cloves garlic, crushed
1 tablespoon grated fresh root
  ginger

2 teaspoons fish sauce
1^{1}/$_{2}$ tablespoons light soy sauce
1 teaspoon crushed palm sugar
1 tablespoon tamarind water, see
  page 27
freshly ground black pepper
coriander sprigs, to garnish

1 Over a medium heat, heat 4 tablespoons oil in a wok. Add fish and fry for about 5 minutes a side until browned and flesh flakes easily when flaked with a knife.

2 Meanwhile, heat remaining oil in a small saucepan over a moderate heat, add onion and cook, stirring occasionally, until browned. When fish is cooked, transfer to absorbent kitchen paper and keep warm.

3 Stir into wok, spring onions, garlic and ginger. Stir-fry for 2–3 minutes, then stir in fish sauce, soy sauce, palm sugar and tamarind water. Cook for 1 minute, season with black pepper, then pour over fish. Sprinkle over the browned onions and garnish with the coriander.

NUTRITIONAL INFORMATION	
Kcal	400
Protein	45g
Carbs	7g
Fat	21g
Salt	1.0g
Sodium	380mg

Fish with Chilli Sauce

[SERVES 2]

1 flat fish, such as pomfret, plump
   plaice or lemon sole, gutted and
   cleaned
vegetable oil for brushing
2 teaspoons vegetable oil
3 small dried red chillies, halved
   lengthwise
2 cloves garlic, finely chopped
1 teaspoon fish sauce
75 ml/2$^{1}/_{2}$ fl oz tamarind water,
   see page 27
1 teaspoon crushed palm sugar
Chilli Flowers, see page 30, to
   garnish

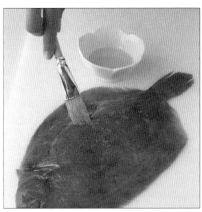

1 Preheat grill. Brush fish lightly with oil, then grill for about 4 minutes a side until lightly coloured and flesh flakes when tested with the point of a knife.

2 Using a fish slice, transfer to a warmed plate and keep warm. In a small saucepan, heat vegetable oil, add chillies and garlic and cook for 1 minute.

3 Stir in remaining ingredients and simmer for 2–3 minutes until lightly thickened. Spoon over fish. Garnish with chilli flowers.

NUTRITIONAL INFORMATION	
Kcal	280
Protein	36g
Carbs	3g
Fat	13g
Salt	1.1g
Sodium	430mg

Fish in Banana Leaf Cups

[SERVES 2]

85 g/3 oz firm white fish, such as cod, hake, monkfish, very finely chopped
85 g/3 oz cooked peeled prawns, very finely chopped
2–3 teaspoons Red Curry Paste, see page 37
2 tablespoons ground peanuts
1 kaffir lime leaf, finely chopped
2 tablespoons coconut milk
1 egg
2 teaspoons fish sauce
leaf part of ½ Chinese cabbage, finely shredded
2 banana leaf cups, see page 31, if desired
2 teaspoons coconut cream, see page 24
strips fresh red chilli or Chilli Flowers, see page 30, to garnish

1 In a bowl, work fish and prawns together using a fork. Mix in curry paste, peanuts and lime leaf. In a small bowl, mix together coconut milk, egg and fish sauce. Stir into fish mixture to evenly combine; set aside for minutes.

2 Divide cabbage leaf between banana cups, or heatproof individual dishes, to make a fine layer. Stir fish mixture and divide between cups or dishes.

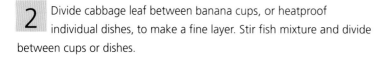

NUTRITIONAL INFORMATION

Kcal	260
Protein	24g
Carbs	5g
Fat	16g
Salt	1.7g
Sodium	650mg

3 Place in a steaming basket and position over a saucepan of boiling water. Cover pan and steam for about 15 minutes until just set in centre. Place on a warmed serving plate, trickle coconut cream over top and garnish.

Barbecued Prawns

[SERVES 4]

vegetable oil for deep-frying
115 g/4 oz rice vermicelli
450 g/1 lb raw unpeeled prawns
2 teaspoons vegetable oil
2–3 spring onions, chopped
2–3 small fresh red chillies,
  chopped
1 tablespoon roasted peanuts,
  crushed coriander sprigs, to
  garnish
Spicy Fish Sauce, see page 47, to
  serve

1 Prepare barbecue or preheat grill. Heat oil for deep-frying to 150C/300F. Break the vermicelli into short strands and deep-fry, a handful at a time, for 30–35 seconds, or until the strands puff up and turn white.

2 Remove vermicelli and drain, then place on a warm serving dish or plate. Cook the prawns on the barbecue, or under the hot grill, turning once; large prawns will take about 6–7 minutes, smaller ones 3–4 minutes to cook. When cooked, arrange them on the bed of crispy rice vermicelli. Heat oil in a small saucepan until hot.

3 Remove from the heat before it starts to smoke, and steep the spring onions and chillies for a few minutes, then pour the mixture all over the prawns. Garnish with crushed peanuts and coriander sprigs and serve hot with the Spicy Fish Sauce as a dip.

NUTRITIONAL INFORMATION	
Kcal	260
Protein	13g
Carbs	23g
Fat	12g
Salt	1.8g
Sodium	690mg

Stir-Fried Prawns

[SERVES 4]

300 g/10 oz raw peeled prawns
3 tablespoons vegetable oil
1 teaspoon chopped garlic
1/2 teaspoon chopped fresh root
    ginger
1 tablespoon chopped spring
    onion
115 g/4 oz straw mushrooms,
    halved lengthways

55 g/2 oz water chestnuts, sliced
3 tablespoons fish sauce
1 tablespoon sugar
about 2–3 tablespoons chicken
    stock or water
1 teaspoon chilli sauce (optional)
salt and freshly ground black
    pepper, to taste
coriander sprigs, to garnish

1 Halve prawns lengthways. Heat oil in a wok or pan and stir-fry the garlic, ginger and spring onion for about 20 seconds. Add the prawns, mushrooms and water chestnuts and stir-fry for about 2 minutes.

2 Add fish sauce and sugar, stir for a few times, then add stock or water. Bring to the boil and stir for another minute or so.

3 Finally, add the chilli sauce, if using, and season with salt and pepper. Garnish with coriander sprigs and serve at once.

VARIATION: This is a standard stir-fry recipe. If preferred, use different types of fish or meat, cut into small, thin slices, and cook with any other kind of vegetables.

NUTRITIONAL INFORMATION	
Kcal	210
Protein	19g
Carbs	10g
Fat	10g
Salt	1.1g
Sodium	440mg

Prawns with Lemon Grass

[SERVES 4]

2 cloves garlic, chopped
1 tablespoon chopped coriander
2 tablespoons chopped lemon
  grass
$1/2$ teaspoon black or white
  peppercorns
3 tablespoons vegetable oil
350–400 g/12–14 oz raw peeled
  prawns, cut in half lengthways
  if large

2 shallots or 1 small onion, sliced
2–3 small fresh chillies, seeded and
  chopped
2–3 tomatoes, cut into wedges
1 tablespoon fish sauce
1 tablespoon oyster sauce
2–3 tablespoons chicken stock or
  water
coriander sprigs, to garnish

1 Using a pestle and mortar, pound the garlic, coriander, lemon grass and peppercorns to a paste.

2 Heat oil in a wok or frying pan and stir-fry the spicy paste for 15–20 seconds until fragrant. Add prawns, shallots or onion, chillies and tomatoes and stir-fry for 2–3 minutes.

3 Add fish sauce, oyster sauce and stock, bring to the boil and simmer for 2–3 minutes. Serve garnished with coriander sprigs.

NUTRITIONAL INFORMATION	
Kcal	200
Protein	18g
Carbs	7g
Fat	11g
Salt	1.4g
Sodium	540mg

Prawns in Yellow Sauce

[SERVES 4]

2 fresh red chillies, seeded and chopped
1 red onion, chopped
1 thick stalk lemon grass, chopped
2.5-cm/1-in piece galangal, chopped
1 teaspoon ground turmeric
250 ml/8 fl oz coconut milk

14–16 raw Mediterranean (king) prawns, peeled and deveined
8 Thai holy basil leaves
2 teaspoons lime juice
1 teaspoon fish sauce
1 spring onion, including some green, cut into fine strips

1 Using a small blender, mix chillies, onion, lemon grass and galangal to a paste. Transfer to a wok and heat, stirring, for 2–3 minutes.

2 Stir in turmeric and 125 ml/4 fl oz water, bring to the boil and simmer for 3–4 minutes until most of the water has evaporated.

3 Stir in coconut milk and prawns and cook gently, stirring occasionally, for about 4 minutes until prawns are just firm and pink. Stir in basil leaves, lime juice and fish sauce. Scatter over strips of spring onion.

NUTRITIONAL INFORMATION	
Kcal	180
Protein	15g
Carbs	6g
Fat	11g
Salt	0.6g
Sodium	250mg

Prawns with Garlic

[SERVES 4]

2 tablespoons vegetable oil
5 cloves garlic, chopped
0.5-cm/$\frac{1}{4}$-in slice fresh root
   ginger, very finely chopped
14–16 large prawns, peeled, tails
   left on
2 teaspoons fish sauce
2 tablespoons chopped coriander
   leaves
freshly ground black pepper
lettuce leaves, lime juice and diced
cucumber, to serve

1   In a wok, heat oil, add garlic and fry until browned.

2   Stir in ginger, heat for 30 seconds, then add prawns and stir-fry for 2–3 minutes until beginning to turn opaque. Stir in fish sauce, coriander, 1–2 tablespoons water and plenty of black pepper. Allow to bubble for 1–2 minutes.

3   Serve prawns on a bed of lettuce leaves with lime juice squeezed over and scattered with cucumber.

NUTRITIONAL INFORMATION	
Kcal	130
Protein	13g
Carbs	1g
Fat	7g
Salt	0.8g
Sodium	330mg

Deep-Fried Coconut Prawns

[SERVES 3–4]

4-cm/1¹/₂-in length cucumber
Dipping Sauce 1, see page 41
8 raw Mediterranean (king)
   prawns
vegetable oil for deep frying
leaves from 1 coriander sprig,
   chopped

BATTER:
115 g/4 oz rice flour
3 tablespoons desiccated coconut
1 egg, separated
185 ml/6 fl oz coconut milk
1 teaspoon fish sauce

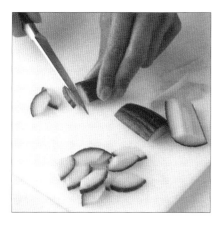

1 Cut cucumber into quarters lengthwise, remove and discard seeds, then thickly slice. Place in a small bowl and add dipping sauce. Set aside. Peel prawns, leaving tails on. Cut along back of each one and remove black spinal cord. Set prawns aside. In a wok, heat oil to 180C/350F.

2 For batter, in a bowl, stir together flour and coconut. Gradually stir in egg yolk, coconut milk and fish sauce. In a bowl, whisk egg white until stiff; fold into batter. Dip prawns in batter to coat them evenly.

3 Deep fry in batches for 2–3 minutes until golden. Using a slotted spoon, transfer to absorbent kitchen paper. Keep warm while frying remainder. Add coriander to sauce and serve with prawns.

NUTRITIONAL INFORMATION	
Kcal	400
Protein	16g
Carbs	30g
Fat	23g
Salt	0.7g
Sodium	260mg

Stir-Fried Prawns and Ginger

[SERVES 3–4]

3 cloves garlic, crushed
4-cm/1½-in piece fresh root
  ginger, thinly sliced
2 tablespoons vegetable oil
12–16 raw Mediterranean (king)
  prawns, peeled and deveined
2 red shallots, finely chopped
grated peel ½ kaffir lime
2 teaspoons fish sauce
3 spring onions, thinly sliced
lime juice, to serve
Spring Onion Brushes, see page
  29, to garnish

1 Using a pestle and mortar or small blender, pound or mix together garlic and ginger. In a wok, heat oil, add garlic paste and stir-fry for 2–3 minutes. Stir in prawns and shallots and stir-fry for 2 minutes.

2 Stir in lime peel, fish sauce and 3 tablespoons water. Allow to bubble for 1 minute until prawns become opaque and cooked through. Stir in spring onions, then remove from heat.

3 Serve in a warmed dish, sprinkled with lime juice and garnished with spring onion brushes.

NUTRITIONAL INFORMATION	
Kcal	200
Protein	15g
Carbs	10g
Fat	11g
Salt	2.5g
Sodium	990mg

Scallops with Lime
[SERVES 3–4]

12 scallops on the half shell
1 tablespoon vegetable oil
2 cloves garlic, chopped
1 red shallot, finely chopped
0.5-cm/¼-in slice galangal, finely chopped
freshly ground black pepper

1 teaspoon finely chopped fresh red chilli
3 tablespoons lime juice
¼ teaspoon crushed palm sugar
1 teaspoon fish sauce
shredded coriander leaves, to garnish

1 Lay scallops on their shells in a steaming basket. In a wok, heat oil, add garlic and shallot and cook, stirring occasionally, until softened. Add galangal and stir for 1 minute.

2 Sprinkle over scallops and grind over black pepper. Cover steaming basket and place over a wok or saucepan of boiling water. Steam for 6-8 minutes until scallops just begin to turn opaque.

3 In a saucepan, gently heat chilli, lime juice, sugar and fish sauce until sugar dissolves. Transfer scallops on their shells to a warmed serving plate, spoon over lime sauce and scatter with coriander.

NUTRITIONAL INFORMATION	
Kcal	260
Protein	47g
Carbs	3g
Fat	7g
Salt	1.7g
Sodium	670mg

Prawns with Mushrooms

[SERVES 3–4]

1 dried red chilli, seeded, soaked in hot water for 20 minutes, drained and chopped
3-cm/1¼-in piece fresh root ginger, chopped
2 cloves garlic, chopped
2 shallots, chopped
1 stalk lemon grass, chopped

1 tablespoon fish sauce
15–20 Thai holy basil leaves
16 raw Mediterranean (king) prawns, peeled with tails left intact, deveined
2–3 large shiitake mushrooms, thinly sliced

1 Using a pestle and mortar or small blender, pound or mix together chilli, ginger, garlic, shallots and lemon grass. Stir in fish sauce and basil leaves.

2 Place prawns in a shallow heatproof bowl and spoon spice mixture over to coat evenly. Add mushrooms. Alternatively, wrap prawns and mushrooms in a banana leaf and secure with wooden cocktail sticks.

3 Place bowl or banana leaf parcel in a steamer above boiling water. Cover and cook for about 8 minutes until the prawns are tender.

NUTRITIONAL INFORMATION	
Kcal	120
Protein	20g
Carbs	5g
Fat	1g
Salt	1.5g
Sodium	580mg

Mussels with Basil

[SERVES 2]

700 g/1¹/₂ lb fresh mussels in shell,
  cleaned, bearded and rinsed
1 large clove garlic, chopped
7.5-cm/3-in piece galangal, thickly
  sliced
2 stalks lemon grass, chopped
10 Thai holy basil sprigs
1 tablespoon fish sauce
Thai holy basil leaves, to garnish
Dipping Sauce 2, see page 43, to
  serve

1 Place mussels, garlic, galangal, lemon grass, basil sprigs and fish sauce in a large saucepan.

2 Add water to a depth of 1 cm/¹/₂ in, cover pan, bring to the boil and cook for about 5 minutes, shaking pan frequently, until mussels have opened; discard any that remain closed.

3 Transfer mussels to a large warmed bowl, or individual bowls, and strain over cooking liquid. Scatter over basil leaves. Serve with sauce to dip mussels into.

NUTRITIONAL INFORMATION	
Kcal	100
Protein	19g
Carbs	2g
Fat	2g
Salt	2.0g
Sodium	780mg

Prawn & Cucumber Curry

[SERVES 3]

4 tablespoons coconut cream, see
  page 24
3-4 tablespoons Red Curry Paste,
  see page 37
225 g/8 oz raw large peeled
  prawns
20-cm/8-in length cucumber,
  halved lengthwise, seeded and
  cut into 2-cm/3/4-in pieces

315 ml/11 fl oz coconut milk
2 tablespoons tamarind water, see
  page 27
1 teaspoon crushed palm sugar
coriander leaves, to garnish

1 In a wok, heat coconut cream, stirring, until it boils, thickens and oil begins to form. Add curry paste.

2 Stir in prawns to coat, then stir in cucumber. Add coconut milk, tamarind water and sugar.

3 Cook gently for about 3–4 minutes until prawns are just cooked through. Transfer to warmed serving dish and garnish with coriander.

NUTRITIONAL INFORMATION	
Kcal	290
Protein	19g
Carbs	7g
Fat	22g
Salt	0.5g
Sodium	210mg

Squid with Spicy Chillies

[SERVES 4–8]

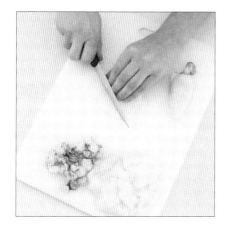

450 g/1 lb fresh squid, cleaned
1/2 teaspoon minced garlic
1/2 teaspoon chopped fresh root
   ginger
salt and freshly ground black
   pepper

1 tablespoon fish sauce
2 tablespoons vegetable oil
2 spring onions, finely shredded
3–4 small red chillies, seeded and
   sliced
coriander sprigs, to garnish

1 Pull the head off each squid, discard head and transparent backbone, but reserve the tentacles. Cut open the body and score the inside of the flesh in a criss-cross pattern.

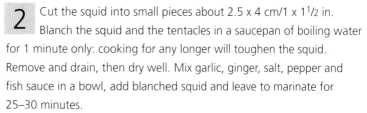

2 Cut the squid into small pieces about 2.5 x 4 cm/1 x 1 1/2 in. Blanch the squid and the tentacles in a saucepan of boiling water for 1 minute only: cooking for any longer will toughen the squid. Remove and drain, then dry well. Mix garlic, ginger, salt, pepper and fish sauce in a bowl, add blanched squid and leave to marinate for 25–30 minutes.

3 Meanwhile, heat the oil in a small saucepan until hot but not smoking. Remove the pan from the heat, add spring onions and chillies and leave to infuse for 15–20 minutes. Arrange the squid with the marinade on a serving plate, pour the oil with the spring onions and chillies all over the squid and garnish with coriander sprigs. Serve cold.

NUTRITIONAL INFORMATION	
Kcal	150
Protein	18g
Carbs	2g
Fat	7g
Salt	1.2g
Sodium	480mg

Seafood Skewers

[SERVES 6]

12 scallops
12 large raw peeled prawns
225 g/8 oz firm white fish fillet,
    such as halibut, cod or monkfish,
    cut into 12 cubes
1 medium onion, cut into 12
    pieces
1 red or green pepper, cut into 12
    cubes
115 ml/4 fl oz dry white wine or
    sherry

1 tablespoon chopped dill
1 tablespoon chopped holy basil
    leaves
1 tablespoon lime juice or vinegar
salt and freshly ground pepper, to
    taste
vegetable oil for brushing
Spicy Fish Sauce, page 47, to serve

1 In a bowl, mix scallops, prawns, fish, onion and pepper with the wine, dill, basil, lime juice or vinegar, salt and pepper. Leave to marinate in a cool place for 2–3 hours, the longer the better.

2 Meanwhile, soak 6 bamboo skewers in hot water for 25–30 minutes and prepare a barbecue or preheat grill. Thread seafood and vegetables alternately onto the skewers so that each skewer has 2 pieces of every ingredient.

3 Brush each filled skewer with a little oil and cook on barbecue or under the hot grill for 5–6 minutes, turning frequently. Serve hot with the fish sauce as a dip.

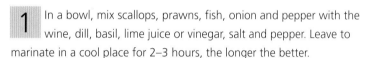

NUTRITIONAL INFORMATION	
Kcal	200
Protein	35g
Carbs	3g
Fat	4g
Salt	0.9g
Sodium	350mg

Spicy Crab
[SERVES 4]

1 clove garlic, chopped
2 shallots or the white parts of
   3–4 spring onions, chopped
1 teaspoon chopped fresh root
   ginger
1 tablespoon chopped lemon
   grass
2–3 tablespoons vegetable oil
1 teaspoon chilli sauce
1 tablespoon sugar
3–4 tablespoons coconut milk

about 450 ml/16 fl oz chicken
   stock
3 tablespoons fish sauce
2 tablespoons lime juice or
   vinegar
meat from 1 large or 2 medium
   cooked crabs, cut into small
   pieces
salt and freshly ground black
   pepper, to taste
coriander sprigs, to garnish

1 Using a pestle and mortar, pound the garlic, shallots or spring onions, ginger and lemon grass to a fine paste. Heat oil in clay pot or flameproof casserole, add the garlic mixture, chilli sauce and sugar and stir-fry for about 1 minute.

2 Add the coconut milk, stock, fish sauce and lime juice or vinegar and bring to the boil. Add the crab pieces and season with salt and pepper. Blend well and cook for 3–4 minutes, stirring constantly.

3 Serve hot, garnished with coriander sprigs.

NOTE: Uncooked crabs can be used for this dish, but increase the cooking time by about 8–10 minutes.

NUTRITIONAL INFORMATION	
Kcal	170
Protein	10g
Carbs	10g
Fat	10g
Salt	2.8g
Sodium	1120mg

Stuffed Squid

[SERVES 4–6]

25 g/1 oz bean thread vermicelli,
  soaked then cut into short
  strands
15 g/¹/₂ oz black fungus, soaked
  then shredded
225 g/8 oz minced lean pork
salt and ground black pepper
2 spring onions, finely chopped
1 tablespoon fish sauce
1 egg, beaten
8–12 small squid, headless
1–2 tablespoons vegetable oil
  lettuce leaves
Spicy Fish Sauce, page 47, as a dip

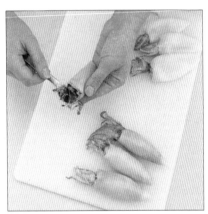

1 In a bowl, mix vermicelli, fungus, pork, salt, pepper, spring onions, fish sauce and egg.

2 Clean the squid and dry well. Fill the squid with the stuffing mixture, then steam them for 25–30 minutes.

3 Remove the squid from the steamer. Heat the oil in a frying pan and fry the stuffed squid for 3–4 minutes, turning once. Serve hot on a bed of lettuce leaves with the Spicy Fish Sauce as a dip.

NOTE: Squid are sometimes available ready cleaned, with tentacles still attached. If wished, the squid can be steamed in advance and then fried just before serving.

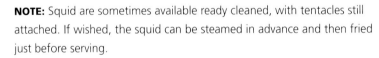

NUTRITIONAL INFORMATION	
Kcal	310
Protein	41g
Carbs	8g
Fat	12g
Salt	1.7g
Sodium	650mg

POULTRY DISHES

Duck Curry

[SERVES 4]

5 tablespoons coconut cream,
  see page 24
5 tablespoons Green Curry
  Paste, see page 35
about 1.35 kg/3 lb duck, skinned
  if desired, well-trimmed of
  excess fat, divided into 8
  portions
625 ml/20 fl oz coconut milk
1 tablespoon fish sauce
8 kaffir lime leaves, shredded
2 fresh green chillies, seeded
  and thinly sliced
12 Thai holy basil leaves
leaves from 5 coriander sprigs
coriander sprigs or Chilli
  Flowers, see page 30, to
  garnish

1 Heat coconut cream in a wok over a medium heat, stirring, until it thickens and oil begins to separate and bubble. Stir in curry paste and cook for about 5 minutes until mixture darkens. Stir in duck pieces to coat with curry mixture.

2 Lower heat, cover and cook for 15 minutes, stirring occasionally. If necessary, using a bulb baster, remove excess fat from the surface, or carefully spoon it off. Stir in coconut milk, fish sauce and lime leaves. Heat to just simmering point, then cook gently without boiling, turning duck over occasionally, for 30–40 minutes until meat is very tender. Remove duck from sauce and allow to stand.

3 Remove surplus fat from surface, then stir in chillies. Cook for a further 5 minutes to thicken sauce. Stir in basil and coriander leaves and cook for a further 2 minutes. Arrange sliced duck on plates and spoon over sauce. Garnish as desired.

NUTRITIONAL INFORMATION

Kcal (Without skin)	490
Protein	40g
Carbs	6g
Fat	35g
Salt	1.3g
Sodium	500mg

Chicken in Coconut Milk

[SERVES 6–8]

8 black peppercorns, cracked
6 coriander roots, finely chopped
4.5-cm/1³/4-in piece galangal, thinly sliced
2 fresh green chillies, seeded and thinly sliced
625 ml/20 fl oz coconut milk
grated peel 1 kaffir lime

4 kaffir lime leaves, shredded
1.35 kg/3 lb chicken, cut into 8 pieces and skinned
1 tablespoon fish sauce
3 tablespoons lime juice
3 tablespoons chopped coriander leaves

1 Using a pestle and mortar or small blender, pound or mix together peppercorns, coriander roots and galangal.

2 In a wok, briefly heat peppercorn mixture, stirring, then stir in chillies, coconut milk, lime peel and leaves. Heat to just simmering point and add chicken portions. Adjust heat so liquid is barely moving, then cook gently for about 40–45 minutes until chicken is very tender and liquid reduced.

3 Stir in fish sauce and lime juice. Scatter coriander leaves over chicken and serve.

NUTRITIONAL INFORMATION	
Kcal	440
Protein	23g
Carbs	3g
Fat	37g
Salt	0.7g
Sodium	270mg

Chicken with Coriander

[SERVES 2–6]

6 coriander sprigs
1 tablespoon black peppercorns, crushed
2 cloves garlic, chopped
juice 1 lime
2 teaspoons fish sauce
4 large or 6 medium chicken drumsticks or thighs
lime wedges, to serve
Spring Onion Brushes, see page 29, to garnish
Carrot Flowers, see page 33, to garnish

1 Using a pestle and mortar or small blender, pound or mix together coriander, peppercorns, garlic, lime juice and fish sauce; set aside.

2 Using the point of a sharp knife, cut slashes in chicken. Spread spice mixture over chicken. Cover and set aside in a cool place for 2–3 hours, turning occasionally.

3 Preheat grill. Grill chicken, basting and turning occasionally, for about 10 minutes until cooked through and golden. Serve with wedges of lime and garnish with spring onion brushes and carrot flowers, it desired..

NUTRITIONAL INFORMATION	
Kcal	260
Protein	27g
Carbs	1g
Fat	17g
Salt	0.5g
Sodium	210mg

Lemon Grass Chicken Curry

[SERVES 3–4]

350 g/12 oz boneless chicken,
  chopped into small pieces
1 tablespoon Red Curry Paste, see
  page 37
3 tablespoons vegetable oil
2 cloves garlic, finely chopped
1 tablespoon fish sauce
2 stalks lemon grass, finely
  chopped
5 kaffir lime leaves, shredded
1/2 teaspoon crushed palm sugar

1 Place chicken in a bowl, add curry paste and stir to coat chicken; set aside for 30 minutes.

2 In a wok, heat oil, add garlic and fry until golden. Stir in chicken, then fish sauce, lemon grass, lime leaves, sugar and 125 ml/ 4 fl oz water.

3 Adjust heat so liquid is barely moving and cook for 15–20 minutes until chicken is cooked through. If chicken becomes too dry, add a little more water, but the final dish should be quite dry.

NUTRITIONAL INFORMATION	
Kcal	280
Protein	24g
Carbs	3g
Fat	19g
Salt	1.4g
Sodium	550mg

Barbecued Chicken

[SERVES 4]

4 fresh red chillies, seeded and
    sliced
2 cloves garlic, chopped
5 shallots, finely sliced
2 teaspoons crushed palm sugar
125 ml/4 fl oz coconut cream,
    see page 24
2 teaspoons fish sauce
1 tablespoon tamarind water,
    see page 27
4 boneless chicken breasts
Thai holy basil leaves or
    coriander leaves, to garnish

1 Using a pestle and mortar or small blender, pound chillies, garlic and shallots to a paste. Work in sugar, then stir in coconut cream, fish sauce and tamarind water.

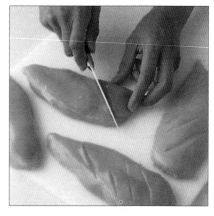

2 Using the point of a sharp knife, cut 4 slashes in chicken breast. Place chicken in a shallow dish and pour over spice mixture. Turn to coat, cover dish and set aside for 1 hour.

3 Preheat grill. Place chicken on a piece of foil and grill for about 4 minutes a side, basting occasionally, until cooked through. Garnish with basil or coriander leaves.

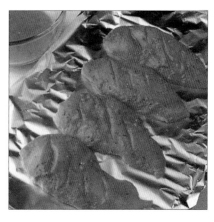

NUTRITIONAL INFORMATION	
Kcal	240
Protein	27g
Carbs	9g
Fat	10g
Salt	0.8g
Sodium	300mg

Spiced Chicken

[SERVES 3–4]

5 shallots, chopped
3 cloves garlic, chopped
5 coriander roots, chopped
2 stalks lemon grass, chopped
2 fresh red chillies, seeded and
    chopped
4-cm/1¹/2 in piece fresh root
    ginger, finely chopped
1 teaspoon shrimp paste
1¹/2 tablespoons vegetable oil
2 skinned chicken legs, divided
    into thighs and drumsticks
1¹/2 tablespoons tamarind
    water, see page 27

1 Using a pestle and mortar or small blender, pound or mix until smooth shallots, garlic, coriander, lemon grass, chillies, ginger and shrimp paste.

2 In a wok, heat oil, stir in spicy paste and cook, stirring, for 3–4 minutes. Stir in chicken pieces to coat evenly.

3 Add tamarind water and 85 ml/3 fl oz water. Cover and cook gently for about 25 minutes until chicken is tender. Garnish with Chilli flowers (see page30) if desired.

NUTRITIONAL INFORMATION	
Kcal	190
Protein	18g
Carbs	7g
Fat	10g
Salt	0.3g
Sodium	100mg

Chicken with Basil

[SERVES 2–3]

2 tablespoons vegetable oil
2 cloves garlic, chopped
350 g/12 oz skinned chicken
   breast, chopped
1 small onion, finely chopped
3 fresh red chillies, seeded and
   thinly sliced
20 Thai holy basil leaves
1 tablespoon fish sauce
4 tablespoons coconut milk
squeeze lime juice
Thai holy basil leaves, to garnish

1 In a wok, heat 1 tablespoon oil, add garlic, chicken, onion and chillies and cook, stirring occasionally, for 3–5 minutes until cooked through.

2 Stir in basil leaves, fish sauce and coconut milk. Stir briefly over heat. Squeeze over lime juice.

3 Serve garnished with basil leaves.

NUTRITIONAL INFORMATION	
Kcal	410
Protein	38g
Carbs	9g
Fat	25g
Salt	1.8g
Sodium	710mg

151

Chicken with Galangal

[SERVES 4]

450 g/1 lb chicken breast meat
3 tablespoons vegetable oil
2 cloves garlic, finely chopped
1 onion, quartered and sliced
2.5-cm/1-in piece galangal, finely chopped
8 pieces dried Chinese black mushrooms, soaked for 30 minutes, drained and chopped

1 fresh red chilli, seeded and cut into fine strips
1 tablespoon fish sauce
1½ teaspoons crushed palm sugar
1 tablespoon lime juice
12 Thai mint leaves
4 spring onions, including some green, chopped
Thai mint leaves, to garnish

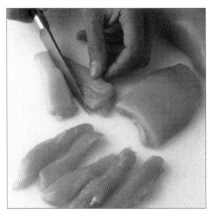

1 Using a sharp knife, cut chicken into 5.5-cm/2½-in long, 2.5-cm/1-in wide pieces; set aside. In a wok, heat oil, add garlic and onion and cook, stirring occasionally, until golden. Stir in chicken and stir-fry for about 2 minutes.

2 Add galangal, mushrooms and chilli and stirfry for 1 minute. Stir in fish sauce, sugar, lime juice, mint leaves, spring onions (scallions) and 3–4 tablespoons water.

3 Cook, stirring, for about 1 minute. Transfer to a warmed serving dish and scatter over mint leaves.

NUTRITIONAL INFORMATION	
Kcal	280
Protein	25g
Carbs	13g
Fat	15g
Salt	1.0g
Sodium	380mg

Chicken in Peanut Sauce

[SERVES 4]

2.5-cm/1-in piece galangal,
  chopped
2 cloves garlic, chopped
1¹/₂ tablespoons Fragrant Curry
  Paste, see page 38
4 tablespoons coconut cream, see
  page 24
450 g/1 lb chicken breast meat, cut
  into large pieces

3 shallots, chopped
4 tablespoons dry-roasted
  peanuts, chopped
250 ml/8 fl oz coconut milk
¹/₂ teaspoon finely chopped dried
  red chilli
2 teaspoons fish sauce
freshly cooked broccoli, to serve

1 Using a pestle and mortar or small blender, pound or mix together galangal, garlic and curry paste. Mix in coconut cream. Place chicken in a bowl and stir in spice mixture; set aside for 1 hour.

2 Heat a wok, add shallots and coated chicken and stir-fry for 3-4 minutes. In a blender, mix peanuts with coconut milk, then stir into chicken with chilli and fish sauce.

3 Cook gently for about 30 minutes until chicken is tender and thick sauce formed. Transfer to centre of a warmed serving plate and arrange cooked broccoli around.

NUTRITIONAL INFORMATION	
Kcal	380
Protein	29g
Carbs	7g
Fat	25g
Salt	0.9g
Sodium	360mg

Chicken with Mangetout

[SERVES 3–4]

3 tablespoons vegetable oil
3 cloves garlic, chopped
1 dried red chilli, seeded and
  chopped
3 red shallots, chopped
2 tablespoons lime juice
2 teaspoons fish sauce
350 g/12 oz chicken, finely
  chopped

1½ stalks lemon grass, chopped
1 kaffir lime leaf, sliced
175 g/6 oz mangetout
1½ tablespoons coarsely ground
  browned rice, see page 27
3 spring onions, chopped
Chilli Flowers, see page 30, and
  sliced spring onions, to garnish

1 In a wok, heat 2 tablespoons oil, add garlic and cook, stirring occasionally, until lightly browned. Stir in chilli, shallots, lime juice, fish sauce and 4 tablespoons water. Simmer for 1–2 minutes, then stir in chicken, lemon grass and lime leaf.

2 Cook, stirring, for 2–3 minutes until chicken is just cooked through. Transfer to a warmed plate and keep warm.

3 Heat remaining oil in wok, add mangetout and stir-fry for 2–3 minutes until just tender. Transfer to a warmed serving plate. Return chicken to wok. Add rice and spring onions. Heat for about 1 minute, then transfer to serving plate. Garnish with chilli flowers and sliced spring onions.

NUTRITIONAL INFORMATION	
Kcal	330
Protein	28g
Carbs	13g
Fat	18g
Salt	0.9g
Sodium	350mg

Steamed Chicken Curry

[SERVES 4]

1 quantity Fragrant Curry Paste,
  see page 38
375 ml/13 fl oz coconut milk
450 g/1 lb chicken breast meat,
  sliced
4 kaffir lime leaves, shredded
8 Thai holy basil leaves
Thai holy basil sprig, to garnish

1 Using a small blender, mix together curry paste, 85 ml/3 fl oz coconut milk and 5 tablespoons water; set aside. Place chicken in a heatproof bowl or dish, stir in remaining coconut milk and set aside for 30 minutes.

2 Stir curry-flavoured coconut milk, lime leaves and basil leaves into bowl or dish. Cover top tightly with foil and place in a steaming basket.

3 Cover with a lid. Position over a saucepan of boiling water. Steam for about 40 minutes until chicken is tender. Garnish with basil.

NOTE: In Thailand the curry is steamed on a bed of lettuce and basil leaves, wrapped in a banana leaf.

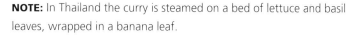

NUTRITIONAL INFORMATION	
Kcal	300
Protein	25g
Carbs	2g
Fat	20g
Salt	0.3g
Sodium	100mg

Chicken with Lemon Grass

[SERVES 4–6]

1.35 kg/3 lb chicken, cut into 8
  pieces
4 thick stalks lemon grass
4 spring onions, chopped
4 black peppercorns, cracked
2 tablespoons vegetable oil
1 fresh green chilli, seeded and
  thinly sliced
2 teaspoons fish sauce
fresh red chilli, cut into thin
  slivers, to garnish

1 With the point of a sharp knife, cut slashes in each chicken piece. Place in a shallow dish.

2 Bruise top parts of each lemon grass stalk and reserve. Chop lower parts, then pound with spring onions and peppercorns using a pestle and mortar. Spread over chicken and into slashes. Cover and set aside for 2 hours.

3 In a wok, heat oil, add chicken and cook, turning occasionally, for about 5 minutes until lightly browned. Add green chilli, bruised lemon grass stalks and 4 tablespoons water. Cover wok and cook slowly for 25–30 minutes until chicken is cooked through. Stir in fish sauce. Transfer chicken pieces to a warmed serving dish, spoon over cooking juices and sprinkle with red chilli.

NUTRITIONAL INFORMATION	
Kcal (including skin)	470
Protein	31g
Carbs	1g
Fat	38g
Salt	0.8g
Sodium	310mg

MEAT DISHES

Beef Curry

[SERVES 3–4]

2 tablespoons vegetable oil
3 tablespoons Red Curry Paste,
  see page 37
350 g/12 oz lean beef, cut into
  cubes
1 stalk lemon grass, finely
  chopped
115 g/4 oz long beans, or green
  beans, cut into 4-cm/1½-in
  lengths
about 8 pieces dried Chinese
  black mushrooms, soaked,
  drained and chopped
3 tablespoons roasted peanuts
1 fresh green chilli, seeded and
  chopped
1 tablespoon fish sauce
2 teaspoons crushed palm sugar
15 Thai mint leaves

1 In a wok, heat oil, add curry paste and stir for 3 minutes. Add beef and lemon grass and stir-fry for 5 minutes. Add beans and mushrooms, stir-fry for 3 minutes, then stir in peanuts and chilli.

2 Stir for 1 minute, then stir in 4 tablespoons water, the fish sauce and sugar and cook for about 2 minutes until beans are tender but crisp.

3 Transfer to a warmed serving dish and scatter over mint leaves. Serve with boiled rice.

NUTRITIONAL INFORMATION	
Kcal	360
Protein	30g
Carbs	11g
Fat	22g
Salt	1.3g
Sodium	510mg

Pork with Water Chestnuts

[SERVES 3–4]

1¹/₂ tablespoons vegetable oil
4 cloves garlic, chopped
2 fresh red chillies, seeded and
  finely chopped
350 g/12 oz lean pork, cubed
10 tinned water chestnuts,
  chopped

1 teaspoon fish sauce
freshly ground black pepper
3 tablespoons chopped coriander
  leaves
6 spring onions, chopped
Spring Onion Brushes, see page
  29, to garnish

1 In a wok, heat oil, add garlic and chillies and cook, stirring
occasionally, until garlic becomes golden.

2 Stir in pork and stir-fry for about 2 minutes until almost cooked
through. Add water chestnuts, heat for 2 minutes, then stir in
fish sauce, 4 tablespoons water and add plenty of black pepper.

3 Stir in coriander and spring onions. Serve garnished with spring
onion brushes.

NUTRITIONAL INFORMATION	
Kcal	260
Protein	26g
Carbs	6g
Fat	15g
Salt	0.6g
Sodium	320mg

Spicy Pork & Lemon Grass

[SERVES 4]

1 clove garlic, chopped
2 shallots, chopped
3 tablespoons chopped lemon grass
1 tablespoon sugar
1 tablespoon fish sauce
salt and freshly ground black pepper, to taste
350 g/12 oz pork fillet, cut into small, thin slices
2–3 tablespoons vegetable oil

2–3 sticks celery, thinly sliced
115 g/4 oz straw mushrooms, halved lengthways
4 small red chillies, seeded and shredded
2 spring onions, shredded
1 tablespoon soy sauce
about 55 ml/2 fl oz stock or water
2 teaspoons cornflour
coriander sprigs, to garnish

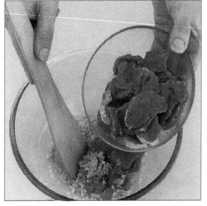

1 Using a pestle and mortar, pound the garlic, shallots and lemon grass to a paste. Transfer to a mixing bowl and add the sugar, fish sauce, salt and pepper. Blend well, then add the pork slices, turning to coat them with the mixture, and leave them to marinate for 25–30 minutes.

2 Heat oil in a wok or frying-pan and stir-fry pork slices for 2 minutes. Add the celery, straw mushrooms, chillies, spring onions and soy sauce and stir-fry for 2–3 minutes.

3 Use the stock to rinse out the marinade bowl and add to the pork. Bring to the boil. Mix cornflour with 1 tablespoon water and add to sauce to thicken it. Garnish with coriander sprigs and serve at once with a mixture of rice and wild rice.

NUTRITIONAL INFORMATION	
Kcal	240
Protein	20g
Carbs	10g
Fat	14g
Salt	0.9g
Sodium	370g

Barbecued Spare Ribs

[SERVES 4–6]

2 tablespoons chopped coriander
  stalks
3 cloves garlic, chopped
1 teaspoon black peppercorns,
  cracked
1 teaspoon grated kaffir lime peel
1 tablespoon Green Curry Paste,
  see page 35

2 teaspoons fish sauce
1½ teaspoons crushed palm sugar
185 ml/6 fl oz coconut milk
900 g/2 lb pork spare ribs,
  trimmed
Spring Onion Brushes, see page
  29, to garnish

1 Using a pestle and mortar or small blender, pound or mix together coriander, garlic, peppercorns, lime peel, curry paste, fish sauce and sugar. Stir in coconut milk.

2 Place spare ribs in a shallow dish and pour over spiced coconut mixture. Cover and leave in a cool place for 3 hours, basting occasionally.

3 Preheat a barbecue or moderate grill. Cook ribs for about 5 minutes a side, until cooked through and brown, basting occasionally with coconut mixture. Garnish with spring onion brushes.

NOTE: The ribs can also be cooked on a rack in a roasting tin in an oven preheated to 200C/400F/Gas Mark 6 for 45–60 minutes, basting occasionally.

NUTRITIONAL INFORMATION	
Kcal	330
Protein	17g
Carbs	6g
Fat	27g
Salt	0.7g
Sodium	270mg

Pork & Bean Stir-Fry

[SERVES 4]

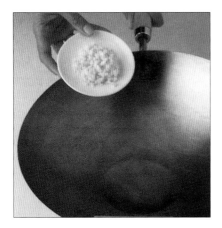

2 tablespoons vegetable oil
6 cloves garlic, chopped
350 g/12 oz lean pork, finely
  chopped
350 g/12 oz long beans or slim
  green beans
12 water chestnuts
115 g/4 oz cooked peeled prawns
1 tablespoon fish sauce
1/2 teaspoon crushed palm sugar
freshly ground black pepper

1 In a wok, heat oil, add garlic and fry, stirring occasionally, until golden.

2 Add pork and beans and stir-fry for 2 minutes, then add water chestnuts. Stir for 1 minute.

3 Add prawns, fish sauce, sugar, plenty of black pepper and about 3 tablespoons water. Bubble for a minute or two, then transfer to a warmed serving plate.

NUTRITIONAL INFORMATION	
Kcal	260
Protein	27g
Carbs	8g
Fat	14g
Salt	2.1g
Sodium	810mg

Thai Pork Curry

[SERVES 3]

125 ml/4 fl oz coconut cream, see
  page 24
1 onion, chopped
1 clove garlic, finely crushed
2 tablespoons Fragrant Curry
  Paste, see page 38
2 teaspoons fish sauce

1/2 teaspoon crushed palm sugar
350 g/12 oz lean pork, diced
3 kaffir lime leaves, shredded
25 Thai holy basil leaves
1 long fresh red chilli, seeded and
  cut into strips, and Thai holy
  basil sprig, to garnish

1 In a wok, heat 85 ml/3 fl oz coconut cream until oil begins to separate. Stir in onion and garlic and cook, stirring occasionally, until lightly browned. Stir in curry paste and continue to stir for about 2 minutes. Stir in fish sauce and sugar, then the pork to coat. Cook for 3–4 minutes.

2 Add lime and basil leaves and cook for 1 more minute. If necessary, add a little water, but final dish should be dry.

3 Garnish with a trail of remaining coconut cream, chilli strips and basil sprig. Serve with boiled rice.

NUTRITIONAL INFORMATION	
Kcal	280
Protein	26g
Carbs	9g
Fat	15g
Salt	1.0g
Sodium	380mg

173

Pork Satay

[SERVES 4]

350 g/12 oz lean pork, cubed
juice 1 lime
1 stalk lemon grass, finely
   chopped
1 clove garlic, chopped
2 tablespoons vegetable oil

SAUCE:
4 tablespoons vegetable oil
85 g/3 oz raw shelled peanuts

2 stalks lemon grass, chopped
2 fresh red chillies, seeded and
   sliced
3 shallots, chopped
2 cloves garlic, chopped
1 teaspoon fish paste
2 teaspoons crushed palm sugar
315 ml/10 fl oz coconut milk juice
1/2 lime

1 Divide pork between 4 skewers and lay them in a shallow dish. In a bowl, mix together lime juice, lemon grass, garlic and oil. Pour over pork, turn to coat, cover and set aside in a cool place for 1 hour, turning occasionally. Preheat grill. Drain excess liquid off pork.

2 Grill, turning frequently and basting, 8–10 minutes. Meanwhile, make sauce. Over a high heat, heat 1 tablespoon oil in a wok, add nuts and cook, stirring constantly, for 2 minutes. Using a slotted spoon, transfer to kitchen paper to drain. Using a pestle and mortar or small blender, grind to a paste. Remove and set aside.

3 Using same, pound or mix lemon grass, chillies, shallots, garlic and fish paste to a smooth paste. Heat remaining oil in wok, add spice mixture and cook, stirring, for 2 minutes. Stir in peanut paste, sugar and coconut milk. Bring to boil, stirring, then adjust heat so sauce simmers. Add lime juice and simmer, stirring, for 5–10 minutes until thickened. Serve in a warmed bowl to accompany pork.

NUTRITIONAL INFORMATION	
Kcal	580
Protein	26g
Carbs	10g
Fat	49g
Salt	0.3g
Sodium	100mg

Pork & Bamboo Shoots

[SERVES 4]

2 tablespoons vegetable oil
4 cloves garlic, very finely
   chopped
350 g/12 oz lean pork, very finely
   chopped
115 g/4 oz canned bamboo
   shoots, chopped or sliced
4 tablespoons peanuts, coarsely
   chopped
2 teaspoons fish sauce
freshly ground black pepper
4 large spring onion, thinly sliced
   Thai holy basil sprig, to garnish

1 In a wok, heat oil, add garlic and fry, stirring occasionally, for about 3 minutes until lightly coloured.

2 Add pork and stir-fry for 2 minutes. Add bamboo shoots and continue to stir for a further minute.

3 Stir in peanuts, fish sauce, plenty of black pepper and half of spring onions. Transfer to a warmed serving plate and sprinkle over remaining spring onions and basil sprig.

NUTRITIONAL INFORMATION	
Kcal	280
Protein	23g
Carbs	3g
Fat	20g
Salt	0.7g
Sodium	260mg

Mixed Vegetables & Pork

[SERVES 4]

225 g/8 oz lean pork, finely
  chopped
freshly ground black pepper
2 tablespoons vegetable oil
3 cloves garlic, finely chopped
450 g/1 lb prepared mixed
  vegetables, such as mangetout,
  broccoli florets, red pepper and
  courgettes
1 tablespoon fish sauce
1/2 teaspoon crushed palm sugar
3 spring onions, sliced

1 In a bowl, mix together pork and plenty of black pepper. Set aside for 30 minutes.

2 In a wok or frying pan, heat oil, add garlic and cook, stirring occasionally, for 2–3 minutes, then stir in pork.

3 Stir briefly until pork changes colour. Stir in mixed vegetables, then fish sauce, sugar and 125 ml/4 fl oz water. Stir for 3–4 minutes until mangetout are bright green and vegetables still crisp. Stir in spring onions.

NUTRITIONAL INFORMATION	
Kcal	190
Protein	15g
Carbs	7g
Fat	11g
Salt	0.8g
Sodium	330mg

Pork with Spring Onions

[SERVES 4–6]

625 ml/21 fl oz coconut milk
450 g/1 lb lean pork, cut into
2.5-cm/1-in cubes
1 tablespoon fish sauce
1/2 teaspoon crushed palm sugar
100 g/3 1/2 oz skinned peanuts
3 fresh red chillies, seeded and
chopped
3-cm/1 1/4-in piece galangal,
chopped

4 cloves garlic
1 stalk lemon grass, chopped
4 tablespoons coconut cream, see
page 24
8 spring onions, chopped
1kg/2 lb young spinach leaves
warmed coconut cream, see page
24, and dry-roasted peanuts, to
serve

1 In a wok, heat coconut milk just to simmering point, adjust heat so liquid barely moves. Add pork and cook for about 25 minutes until very tender.

2 Meanwhile, using a small blender or food processor, mix fish sauce, sugar, peanuts, chillies, galangal, garlic and lemon grass to a paste. In another wok, or a frying pan, heat coconut cream until oil separates. Add spring onions and peanut paste and cook, stirring frequently, for 2–3 minutes.

3 Stir in milk from pork and boil until lightly thickened. Pour over pork, stir and cook for 5 minutes more. Rinse spinach leaves, then pack into a saucepan with just water left on them. Gently cook for about 3 minutes until just beginning to wilt. Arrange on a warmed serving plate. Spoon pork and sauce onto centre. Trickle over coconut cream and scatter over dry-roasted peanuts.

NUTRITIONAL INFORMATION	
Kcal (not extra cream/nuts)	600
Protein	34g
Carbs	9g
Fat	47g
Salt	0.9g
Sodium	370mg

RICE &
NOODLES

Noodles, Pork & Prawns

[SERVES 4]

200 g/7 oz bean thread noodles
6 dried Chinese black
   mushrooms
2 tablespoons vegetable oil
350 g/12 oz lean pork, very
   finely chopped
115 g/4 oz cooked peeled large
   prawns
3 red shallots, finely chopped
4 spring onions, including some
   green, sliced
3 slim inner celery stalks, thinly
   sliced
55 g/2 oz dried shrimps
2 tablespoons fish sauce
5 tablespoons lime juice
1$\frac{1}{2}$ teaspoons crushed palm
   sugar
2 fresh red chillies, seeded and
   sliced
15 g/$\frac{1}{2}$ oz coriander leaves,
   chopped
whole cooked prawns and
   coriander, to garnish

NUTRITIONAL INFORMATION

Kcal	510
Protein	41g
Carbs	51g
Fat	17g
Salt	2.8g
Sodium	110mg

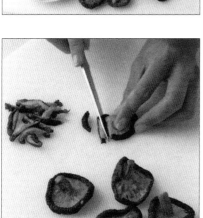

1   Soak noodles in cold water for 15 minutes. Soak mushrooms in water for 30 minutes. Drain and chop. In a wok, heat oil, add pork and stir-fry for 2–3 minutes until cooked through.

2   Using a slotted spoon, transfer to absorbent kitchen paper. Add noodles to a saucepan of boiling water and boil for 5 minutes. Drain well and set aside.

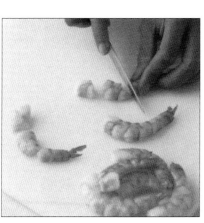

3   Cut each prawn into 3 and place in a bowl. Add shallots, spring onions, celery, mushrooms, noodles, pork and dried shrimps; toss together. In a small bowl, mix together fish sauce, lime juice and sugar. Pour into bowl, add coriander leaves and toss ingredients together. Serve garnished with whole prawns and coriander sprigs.

Crispy Noodles

[SERVES 4]

175 g/6 oz rice vermicelli
6 pieces dried Chinese black
  mushrooms
115 g/4 oz lean pork
115 g/4 oz chicken breast
  vegetable oil for deep frying
2 eggs
4 cloves garlic, finely chopped
3 shallots, thinly sliced

1 fresh red and 1 fresh green chilli,
  seeded and sliced
6 tablespoons lime juice
1 tablespoon fish sauce
1 tablespoon crushed palm sugar
45 g/1¹/2 oz cooked peeled
  shrimps
115 g/4 oz beansprouts
3 spring onions, thickly sliced

1 Soak vermicelli in water for 20 minutes, drain and set aside. Soak mushrooms in water for 20 minutes, drain, chop and set aside. Cut pork and chicken into 2.5-cm/1-in strips. Set aside. For garnish, heat 2 teaspoons oil in a wok. In a bowl, beat eggs with 2 tablespoons water, then drip small amounts in batches in tear shapes onto wok.

2 Cook for 1¹/2–2 minutes until set. Remove using a fish slice or thin spatula. Set aside. Add more oil to wok for deep frying. Heat to 190C/375F. Add vermicelli in batches and fry until puffed, light golden brown and crisp. Transfer to absorbent kitchen paper. Set aside.

3 Pour off oil leaving 3 tablespoons. Add garlic and shallots and cook, stirring occasionally, until lightly browned. Add pork, stir-fry for 1 minute, then mix in chicken arid stir for 2 minutes. Stir in chillies, mushrooms, lime juice, fish sauce and sugar. Bubble until liquid becomes very lightly syrupy. Add shrimps, beansprouts and noodles, tossing to coat with sauce without breaking up noodles. Serve with spring onions scattered over and garnished with egg tears.

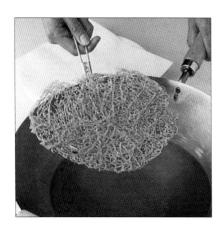

NUTRITIONAL INFORMATION	
Kcal	550
Protein	24g
Carbs	47g
Fat	30g
Salt	1.4g
Sodium	560mg

Thai Fried Noodles

[SERVES 4]

3 tablespoons vegetable oil
4 cloves garlic, crushed
1 tablespoon fish sauce
3–4 tablespoons lime juice
1 teaspoon crushed palm sugar
2 eggs, beaten
350 g/12 oz rice vermicelli, soaked
   in water for 20 minutes, drained
115 g/4 oz cooked peeled shrimps

115 g/4 oz beansprouts
4 spring onions, sliced
2 tablespoons ground dried
   shrimps, finely chopped roasted
   peanuts, coriander leaves and
   lime slices, to garnish

1 In a wok, heat oil, add garlic and cook, stirring occasionally, until golden. Stir in the fish sauce, lime juice and sugar until the sugar has dissolved.

2 Quickly stir in eggs and cook for a few seconds. Stir in noodles to coat with garlic and egg, then add shrimps, 85g/3 oz of the beansprouts and half spring onions.

3 When noodles are tender, transfer contents of wok to a warmed serving dish. Garnish with remaining beansprouts and spring onions, dried shrimps, peanuts, coriander leaves and lime slices.

NUTRITIONAL INFORMATION	
Kcal (Not peanuts)	520
Protein	23g
Carbs	74g
Fat	14g
Salt	2.0g
Sodium	800mg

Noodles with Herb Sauce

[SERVES 4]

75 ml/2¹/2 fl oz vegetable oil
2 tablespoons raw shelled peanuts
1 small fresh green chilli, seeded
  and sliced
2-cm/¹/2 in piece galangal,
  chopped
2 large cloves garlic, chopped
leaves from bunch Thai holy basil
  (about 90)

leaves from small bunch Thai mint
  (about 30)
leaves from small bunch coriander
  (about 40)
2 tablespoons lime juice
1 teaspoon fish sauce
350–450 g/12–16 oz egg noodles,
  soaked for 5–10 minutes

1 Over a high heat, heat oil in a wok, add peanuts and cook, stirring, for about 2 minutes until browned. Using a slotted spoon, transfer nuts to absorbent kitchen paper to drain; reserve oil.

2 Using a small blender, roughly grind nuts. Add chilli, galangal and garlic. Mix briefly. Add the herbs, lime juice, fish sauce and reserved oil.

3 Drain noodles, shake loose, then cook in a pan of boiling salted water for 2 minutes until soft. Drain well, turn into a warmed dish and toss with sauce.

NUTRITIONAL INFORMATION	
Kcal	530
Protein	13g
Carbs	71g
Fat	22g
Salt	2.4g
Sodium	930mg

Noodles, Crab & Aubergine

[SERVES 3]

225 g/8 oz brown and white crabmeat
175 g/6 oz dried egg thread noodles
3 tablespoons vegetable oil
1 aubergine, about 225 g/8 oz, cut into about 5 x 0.5-cm/2 x 1/4-in strips
2 cloves garlic, very finely chopped

1-cm/1/2-in slice galangal, finely chopped
1 fresh green chilli, seeded and finely chopped
6 spring onions, sliced
1 tablespoon fish sauce
2 teaspoons lime juice
1 1/2 tablespoons chopped coriander leaves

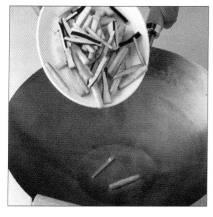

1 In a bowl, mash brown crab meat well. Roughly mash white meat. Set aside.

2 Add noodles to a saucepan of boiling salted water and cook for about 4 minutes until just tender. Drain well. Meanwhile, in a wok, heat 2 tablespoons oil, add aubergine and stir-fry for about 5 minutes until evenly well coloured. Using a slotted spoon, transfer to absorbent kitchen paper; set aside.

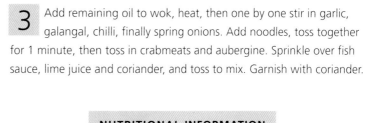

3 Add remaining oil to wok, heat, then one by one stir in garlic, galangal, chilli, finally spring onions. Add noodles, toss together for 1 minute, then toss in crabmeats and aubergine. Sprinkle over fish sauce, lime juice and coriander, and toss to mix. Garnish with coriander.

NUTRITIONAL INFORMATION	
Kcal	430
Protein	22g
Carbs	50g
Fat	18g
Salt	2.0g
Sodium	790mg

Noodles with Broccoli

[SERVES 4]

450 g/1 lb wet rice noodles
225 g/8 oz broccoli
2 tablespoons vegetable oil
3 cloves garlic, finely chopped
225 g/8 oz lean pork, finely
  chopped
4 tablespoons roasted peanuts,
  chopped
2 teaspoons fish sauce
$1/2$ teaspoon crushed palm sugar
1 fresh red chilli, seeded and cut
  into thin slivers, to garnish

1 Remove wrapping from noodles and immediately cut into 1-cm/$1/2$-in strips; set aside. Cut broccoli diagonally into 5-cm/2-in wide pieces and cook in a saucepan of boiling salted water for 2 minutes. Drain, then refresh under cold running water and drain well; set aside.

2 In a wok, heat oil, add garlic and fry, stirring occasionally, until golden. Using a slotted spoon, transfer to absorbent kitchen paper; set aside. Add pork to wok and stir-fry for 2 minutes.

3 Add noodles, stir quickly, then add broccoli and peanuts and stir-fry for 2 minutes. Stir in fish sauce, sugar and 3 tablespoons water. Stir briefly and serve garnished with the reserved garlic and the chilli slivers.

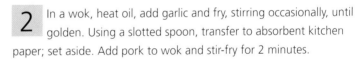

NUTRITIONAL INFORMATION	
Kcal	320
Protein	21g
Carbs	18g
Fat	19g
Salt	0.6g
Sodium	240mg

Rice, Prawns & Bean Curd

[SERVES 4]

175 g/6 oz long-grain white rice
3 tablespoons vegetable oil
3 cloves garlic, chopped
1 small onion, chopped
115 g/4 oz bean curd, drained and
  cut into about 1-cm/½-in cubes
2 small fresh red chillies, seeded
  and finely chopped

1 tablespoon fish sauce
175 g/6 oz peeled prawns
1 shallot, thinly sliced
Chilli Flower, see page 30, and
  coriander leaves, to garnish

1 Cook rice, see page 27. In a wok, heat the oil, add garlic and onion and cook, stirring occasionally, for 3–4 minutes until lightly browned.

2 Add bean curd and fry for about 3 minutes until browned. Add chillies and stir-fry briefly. Stir in fish sauce and rice for 2–3 minutes, then stir in prawns.

3 Add shallot, stir quickly to mix, then transfer to a warmed serving plate. Garnish with chilli flower and scatter coriander leaves over rice mixture.

NUTRITIONAL INFORMATION	
Kcal	330
Protein	14g
Carbs	41g
Fat	12g
Salt	0.9g
Sodium	380mg

Spicy Fried Rice

[SERVES 4]

175 g/6 oz long-grain white rice
2 tablespoons vegetable oil
1 large onion, finely chopped
3 cloves garlic, chopped
2 fresh green chillies, seeded and
  finely chopped
2 tablespoons Red Curry Paste, see
  page 37

55 g/2 oz lean pork, very finely
  chopped
3 eggs, beaten
1 tablespoon fish sauce
55 g/2 oz cooked peeled prawns
finely sliced red chilli, shredded
  coriander leaves and Spring
  Onion Brushes (see page 29), to
  garnish

1 Cook rice, see page 12. In a wok, heat oil, add onion, garlic and chillies and cook, stirring occasionally, until onion has softened. Stir in curry paste and continue to stir for 3–4 minutes.

2 Add pork and stir-fry for 2–3 minutes. Stir in rice to coat with ingredients, then push to sides of wok.

3 Pour eggs into centre of wok. When just beginning to set, mix evenly into the rice, adding fish sauce at the same time. Stir in prawns, then transfer to a shallow, warmed serving dish. Garnish with chilli, coriander and spring onion brushes.

NUTRITIONAL INFORMATION	
Kcal	350
Protein	18g
Carbs	41g
Fat	14g
Salt	1.6g
Sodium	630mg

Thai Fried Rice

[SERVES 4]

175 g/6 oz long-grain white rice
115 g/4 oz long beans, or French
  beans, cut into 2.5-cm/1-in
  lengths
3 tablespoons vegetable oil
2 onions, finely chopped
3 cloves garlic, crushed
85 g/3 oz lean pork, very finely
  chopped
85 g/3 oz chicken breast meat,
  very finely chopped

2 eggs, beaten
2 tablespoons Nam Prik, see page
  44
1 tablespoon fish sauce
85 g/3 oz cooked peeled prawns
coriander leaves, sliced spring
  onions and lime wedges, to
  garnish

1 Cook rice, see page 27. Add beans to a saucepan of boiling water and cook for 2 minutes. Drain and refresh under cold running water. Drain well.

2 In a wok, heat oil, add onions and garlic and cook, stirring occasionally, until softened. Stir in pork and chicken and stir-fry for 1 minute. Push to side of wok.

3 Pour eggs into centre of wok, leave until just beginning to set, then stir in pork mixture followed by nam prik, fish sauce and rice. Stir for 1–2 minutes, then add beans and prawns. Serve garnished with coriander leaves, spring onions and lime wedges.

NUTRITIONAL INFORMATION	
Kcal	460
Protein	32g
Carbs	45g
Fat	16g
Salt	4.0g
Sodium	1610mg

Rice, Chicken & Mushrooms

[SERVES 4]

175 g/6 oz long-grain white rice
2 tablespoons vegetable oil
1 small onion, finely chopped
2 cloves garlic, finely chopped
2 fresh red chillies, seeded and cut
  into slivers
225 g/8 oz chicken breast meat,
  finely chopped
85 g/3 oz bamboo shoots,

chopped or cut into matchstick
  strips
8 pieces dried Chinese black
  mushrooms, soaked for 30
  minutes; drained and chopped
2 tablespoons dried shrimps
1 tablespoon fish sauce
about 20 Thai holy basil leaves
Thai holy basil sprig, to garnish

1 Cook rice, see page 27. In a wok, heat oil, add onion and garlic
   and cook, stirring occasionally, until golden.

2 Add chillies and chicken and stir-fry for 2 minutes. Stir in bamboo
   shoots, mushrooms, dried shrimps and fish sauce.

3 Continue to stir for 2 minutes, then stir in rice and basil. Serve
   garnished with basil sprig.

NUTRITIONAL INFORMATION	
Kcal	330
Protein	18g
Carbs	43g
Fat	9g
Salt	0.8g
Sodium	330mg

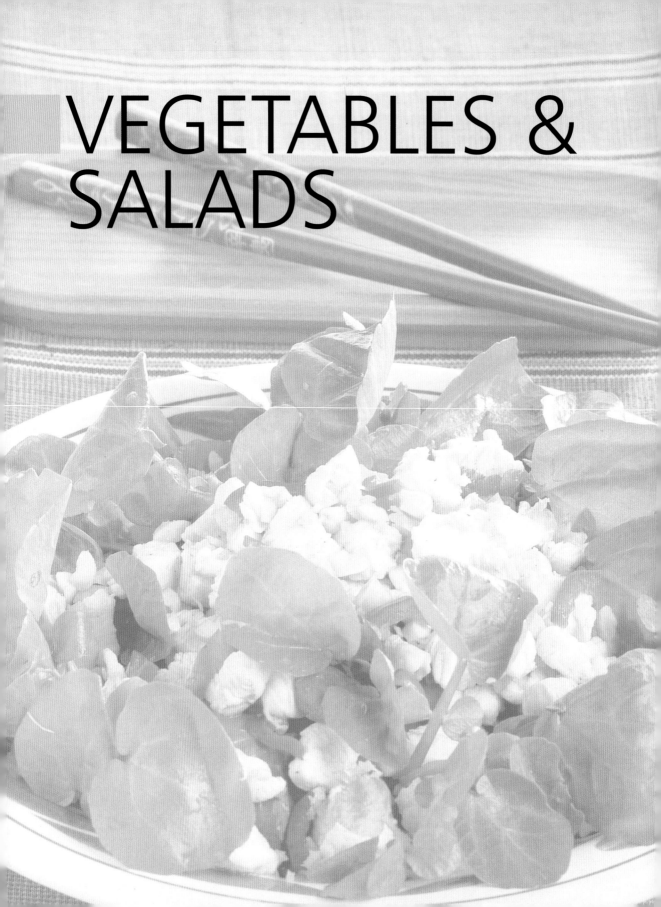

VEGETABLES & SALADS

Stuffed Aubergine

[SERVES 4]

2 aubergines, each about
225 g/8 oz
2 cloves garlic, finely chopped
2 stalks lemon grass, chopped
2 tablespoons vegetable oil
1 small onion, finely chopped
175 g/6 oz chicken breast meat,
  finely chopped
2 teaspoons fish sauce
about 20 Thai holy basil leaves
freshly ground black pepper
Thai holy basil leaves, to garnish

1 Preheat grill. Place aubergines under grill and cook, turning as necessary, for about 20 minutes until evenly charred.

2 Meanwhile, using a pestle and mortar, pound together garlic and lemon grass; set aside. Heat oil in a wok, add onion and cook, stirring occasionally, until lightly browned. Stir in garlic mixture, cook for 1–2 minutes, then add chicken. Stir-fry for 2 minutes. Stir in fish sauce, basil leaves and plenty of black pepper.

3 Using a sharp knife, slice each charred aubergine in half lengthways. Using a teaspoon, carefully scoop aubergine flesh into a bowl; keep skins warm. Using kitchen scissors, chop flesh. Add to wok and stir ingredients together for about 1 minute. Place aubergine skins on a large warmed plate and divide chicken mixture between them. Garnish with basil leaves.

NUTRITIONAL INFORMATION	
Kcal	150
Protein	11g
Carbs	6g
Fat	9g
Salt	0.6g
Sodium	230mg

Stir-Fried Mangetout

[SERVES 4–6]

2 tablespoons vegetable oil
3 cloves garlic, finely chopped
115 g/4 oz lean pork, very finely
  chopped
450 g/1 lb mangetout
1/2 teaspoon crushed palm sugar
1 tablespoon fish sauce
55 g/2 oz cooked peeled prawns,
  chopped
freshly ground black pepper

1 In a wok, heat oil over a medium heat, add garlic and fry until lightly coloured. Add pork and stir-fry for 2–3 minutes.

2 Add mangetout and stir-fry for about 3 minutes until cooked but still crisp.

3 Stir in sugar, fish sauce, prawns and black pepper. Heat briefly and serve.

NUTRITIONAL INFORMATION	
Kcal	160
Protein	13g
Carbs	7g
Fat	9g
Salt	1.3g
Sodium	520mg

Broccoli with Prawns

[SERVES 4]

3 tablespoons peanut oil
4 cloves garlic, finely chopped
1 fresh red chilli, seeded and
  thinly sliced
450g/1 lb trimmed broccoli, cut
  diagonally into 2.5-cm/1-in slices
115 g/4 oz cooked peeled shrimps
1 tablespoon fish sauce
½ teaspoon crushed palm sugar

1 In a wok, heat oil, add garlic and fry, stirring occasionally, until just beginning to colour. Add chilli and cook for 2 minutes.

2 Quickly stir in broccoli. Stir-fry for 3 minutes. Reduce heat, cover wok and cook for 4–5 minutes until broccoli is cooked but still crisp.

3 Remove lid, stir in shrimps, fish sauce and sugar. Serve immediately on warm plates.

NUTRITIONAL INFORMATION	
Kcal	160
Protein	12g
Carbs	4g
Fat	11g
Salt	1.9g
Sodium	750mg

Spiced Cabbage

[SERVES 4]

14 black peppercorns
2 tablespoons coconut cream,
 see page 24
2 shallots, chopped
115 g/4 oz lean pork, very finely
 chopped
about 450 g/1 lb white
 cabbage, finely sliced
315 ml/10 fl oz coconut milk
1 tablespoon fish sauce
1 fresh red chilli, seeded and
 very finely chopped

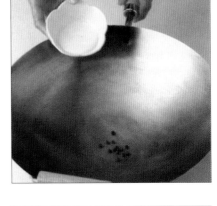

1 In a wok, heat the peppercorns for about 3 minutes until the aroma changes. Stir in coconut cream, heat for 2–3 minutes, then stir in the shallots.

2 Stir-fry for a further 2–3 minutes, then stir in pork and cabbage. Cook, stirring occasionally, for 3 minutes, then add coconut milk and bring just to the boil. Cover and simmer for 5 minutes.

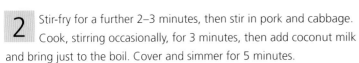

3 Uncover and cook for about 10 minutes until the cabbage is tender but retains some bite. Stir in the fish sauce. Serve sprinkled with chilli.

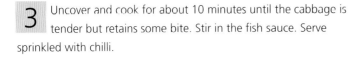

NUTRITIONAL INFORMATION	
Kcal	220
Protein	10g
Carbs	10g
Fat	16g
Salt	0.8g
Sodium	310mg

Vegetables with Sauce

[SERVES 6]

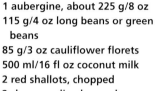

1 aubergine, about 225 g/8 oz
115 g/4 oz long beans or green
  beans
85 g/3 oz cauliflower florets
500 ml/16 fl oz coconut milk
2 red shallots, chopped
2 cloves garlic, chopped
4 coriander roots, chopped
2 dried red chillies, seeded and
  chopped
1 stalk lemon grass, chopped
3-cm/1^{1}/$_{4}$-in piece galangal,
  chopped
grated peel 1 kaffir lime
4 tablespoons coconut cream,
  see page 24
1^{1}/$_{2}$ tablespoons ground roasted
  peanuts
3 tablespoons tamarind water,
  see page 27
1 tablespoon fish sauce
2 teaspoons crushed palm
  sugar

NUTRITIONAL INFORMATION

Kcal	200
Protein	4g
Carbs	8g
Fat	17g
Salt	0.5g
Sodium	190mg

1 Cut aubergine into 4-cm/1^{1}/$_{2}$-in cubes; cut beans into 5-cm/2-in lengths. Put aubergine, beans and cauliflower into a saucepan, add coconut milk and bring to the boil. Cover and simmer for 10 minutes until vegetables are tender.

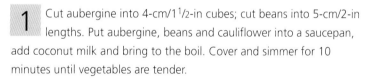

2 Remove from heat, uncover and set aside. Using a pestle and mortar or small blender, pound or mix together shallots, garlic, coriander roots, chillies, lemon grass, galangal and lime peel.

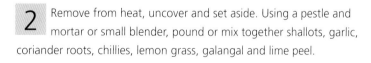

3 Mix in 4 tablespoons liquid from the vegetables. Place in a small, heavy frying pan, stir in coconut cream and heat, stirring, until oil is released and paste is thick. Stir into vegetables with peanuts, tamarind water, fish sauce and sugar. Heat through gently for about 1 minute.

Mushrooms & Bean Sprouts

[SERVES 4]

2 tablespoons vegetable oil
2 fresh red chillies, seeded and
  thinly sliced
2 cloves garlic, chopped
225 g/8 oz shiitake mushrooms,
  sliced
115 g/4 oz beansprouts
115 g/4 oz cooked peeled prawns
2 tablespoons lime juice

2 red shallots, sliced into rings
1 tablespoon fish sauce
1/2 teaspoon crushed palm sugar
1 tablespoon ground browned
  rice, see page 27
6 coriander sprigs, stalks and
  leaves finely chopped
10 Thai mint leaves, shredded
Thai mint leaves, to garnish

1 In a wok, heat oil, add chillies and garlic and cook, stirring occasionally, for 2–3 minutes. Add mushrooms and stir-fry for 2–3 minutes.

2 Add beansprouts and prawns, stir-fry for 1 minute, then stir in lime juice, shallots, fish sauce and sugar.

3 When hot, remove from heat and stir in rice, coriander and mint. Serve garnished with mint leaves.

NUTRITIONAL INFORMATION	
Kcal	140
Protein	9g
Carbs	9g
Fat	8g
Salt	1.9g
Sodium	740mg

Tossed Spinach

[SERVES 4]

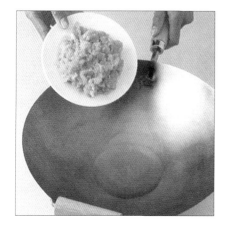

2 tablespoons peanut oil
225 g/8 oz chicken breast meat,
  very finely chopped
6 cloves garlic, finely chopped
700 g/1^1/$_2$ lb spinach leaves, torn
  into large pieces if necessary
1^1/$_2$ tablespoons fish sauce
freshly ground black pepper
1^1/$_2$ tablespoons dry-fried
  unsalted peanuts, chopped
thinly sliced fresh seeded chilli, to
  garnish

1 In a wok, heat oil, add chicken and stir-fry for 2–3 minutes. Using a slotted spoon, transfer to absorbent kitchen paper; set aside.

2 Add garlic to wok and fry until just coloured. Using slotted spoon, transfer half to absorbent kitchen paper; set aside. Increase heat beneath wok so oil is lightly smoking. Quickly add all spinach, stir briefly to coat with oil and garlic.

3 Scatter chicken over, sprinkle with fish sauce and pepper. Reduce heat, cover wok and simmer for 2–3 minutes. Scatter over peanuts and reserved garlic and garnish with sliced chilli. Serve immediately.

NUTRITIONAL INFORMATION	
Kcal	210
Protein	18g
Carbs	6g
Fat	13g
Salt	1.7g
Sodium	670mg

Chicken & Mint Salad

[SERVES 4]

1 stalk lemon grass, finely
    chopped
2–3 fresh red chillies, seeded and
    finely chopped
3 tablespoons lime juice
1 tablespoon fish sauce
2 teaspoons crushed palm sugar
1¹/₂ tablespoons vegetable oil
450 g/1 lb skinless chicken breast
    meat, very finely chopped
15 Thai mint leaves, shredded
lettuce leaves, to serve
mint sprig and Chilli Flowers, see
    page 30, to garnish

1 In a bowl, mix together lemon grass, chillies, lime juice, fish sauce and sugar; set aside.

2 In a wok, heat oil, stir in chicken and cook over a fairly high heat, stirring, for about 1¹/₂ minutes until cooked through. Using a slotted spoon, quickly transfer to absorbent kitchen paper to drain, then add to bowl.

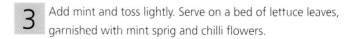

3 Add mint and toss lightly. Serve on a bed of lettuce leaves, garnished with mint sprig and chilli flowers.

NUTRITIONAL INFORMATION	
Kcal	200
Protein	23g
Carbs	4g
Fat	10g
Salt	0.9g
Sodium	370mg

Spicy Chicken Salad

[SERVES 4–6]

225–300 g/8–10 oz boneless
  cooked chicken meat, shredded
1/2 cucumber, thinly shredded
1 carrot and 1 small onion, thinly
  shredded
salt and freshly ground black
  pepper
few lettuce leaves
2 small red chillies, seeded and
  shredded
1 tablespoon roasted peanuts,
  crushed
coriander sprigs, to garnish

DRESSING:
1 clove garlic, chopped
1 teaspoon chopped fresh root
  ginger
1–2 small red or green chillies,
  chopped
1 tablespoon palm sugar
2 tablespoons each fish sauce and
  lime juice
1 tablespoon sesame oil

1 In a bowl, mix together chicken, cucumber, carrot and onion and season with salt and pepper. Arrange a bed of lettuce leaves on a serving dish or plate and spoon the chicken mixture on top.

2 Using a pestle and mortar, pound the garlic, ginger, chillies and sugar to a fine paste, then blend the paste with the rest of the dressing ingredients.

3 Pour the dressing all over the salad just before serving, and garnish with the chillies, peanuts and coriander sprigs.

NOTE: Do not toss and mix the salad with the dressing until you are ready to serve.

NUTRITIONAL INFORMATION	
Kcal	180
Protein	16g
Carbs	12g
Fat	8g
Salt	1.6g
Sodium	630mg

Cucumber Salad

[SERVES 3–4]

2 tablespoons vegetable oil
2 tablespoons shelled peanuts
1 large cucumber, peeled
1 small fresh red chilli, seeded and
   thinly sliced
1 small fresh green chilli, seeded
   and thinly sliced
1 shallot, finely chopped

2 teaspoons finely chopped kaffir
   lime peel
1½ tablespoons lime juice
2 teaspoons fish sauce
1 teaspoon crushed palm sugar
about 15 dried shrimps, finely
   chopped

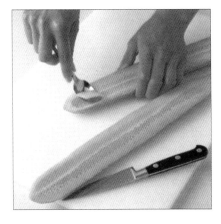

1 In a wok, heat oil until very hot, add peanuts and cook, stirring, for 2–3 minutes until lightly browned.

2 Using a slotted spoon, transfer to absorbent kitchen paper to drain; set aside. Cut cucumber in half lengthways, scoop out and discard seeds. Cut into small chunks and place in a bowl; set aside.

3 Mix together chillies, shallot, lime peel, lime juice, fish sauce and sugar. Pour over cucumber and toss lightly. Chop peanuts and scatter over salad with chopped shrimps.

NUTRITIONAL INFORMATION	
Kcal	220
Protein	13g
Carbs	9g
Fat	14g
Salt	0.7g
Sodium	260mg

Prawn Salad with Mint

[SERVES 3–4]

16–20 raw large prawns, peeled and deveined
juice 2 limes
2 teaspoons vegetable oil
2 teaspoons crushed palm sugar
2 tablespoons tamarind water, see page 27
1 tablespoon fish sauce
2 teaspoons Red Curry Paste, see page 37

2 stalks lemon grass, very finely chopped
4 tablespoons coconut cream, see page 24
10 Thai mint leaves, shredded
5 kaffir lime leaves, shredded
1 small crisp lettuce, divided into leaves
1 small cucumber, thinly sliced
Thai mint leaves, to garnish

1 Put prawns in a bowl, pour over lime juice and leave for 30 minutes. Remove prawns, allowing excess liquid to drain into bowl; reserve liquid.

2 Heat oil in a wok, add prawns and stir-fry for 2–3 minutes until just cooked: marinating in lime juice speeds up the process. Meanwhile, stir sugar, tamarind water, fish sauce, curry paste, lemon grass, coconut cream, mint and lime leaves into reserved lime liquid. Stir in cooked prawns. Set aside until cold.

3 Make a bed of lettuce on a serving plate, place on a layer cucumber slices. Spoon prawns and dressing on top. Garnish with mint leaves.

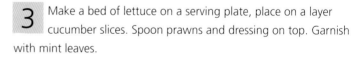

NUTRITIONAL INFORMATION	
Kcal	140
Protein	10g
Carbs	8g
Fat	6g
Salt	1.3g
Sodium	530mg

Squid Salad

[SERVES 3–4]

450 g/1 lb small or medium squid
2 tablespoons vegetable oil
1/2 small red pepper, seeded and halved lengthways
1 tablespoon fish sauce
3 tablespoons lime juice
1 teaspoon crushed palm sugar
2 cloves garlic, very finely crushed
1 stalk lemon grass, very finely chopped
1 fresh red chilli, seeded and thinly sliced
10 Thai mint leaves, cut into strips
2 tablespoons chopped coriander leaves
2 spring onions, chopped
1 cucumber, peeled, if desired, thinly sliced
coriander sprigs, to garnish

NUTRITIONAL INFORMATION

Kcal	220
Protein	24g
Carbs	7g
Fat	10g
Salt	1.6g
Sodium	640mg

1   Clean squid. Holding head just below eyes, pull away from body pouch. Discard soft innards. Carefully remove ink sac. Pull quill-shaped pen free from pouch. Slip fingers under skin on body pouch and slip it off. Cut off edible fins on either side of pouch. Cut off tentacles just below eyes; discard head. Squeeze out beak-like mouth. Discard.

2   Rinse tentacles, pouch and fins thoroughly. Dry well, then slice into rings. Heat oil in a wok, add squid and fry gently, stirring occasionally, for about 10–15 minutes until tender. Transfer to kitchen paper to drain. Meanwhile, chargrill red pepper and remove skin.

3   Seed and roughly chop pepper. In a bowl, mix together fish sauce, lime juice, sugar and garlic. Add squid and mix together, then toss with lemon grass, chilli, red pepper, mint, chopped coriander and spring onions. Place on cucumber slices and garnish with coriander.

Thai Beef Salad

[SERVES 3–4]

350 g/12 oz lean beef, very
  finely chopped
1 tablespoon fish sauce
2 tablespoons lime juice
2 teaspoons crushed palm sugar
1¹/₂ tablespoons long-grain
  white rice, browned and
  coarsely ground, see page 27
2 fresh green chillies, seeded
  and finely chopped
2 cloves garlic, finely chopped
8 Thai mint leaves
4 kaffir lime leaves, torn
8 Thai holy basil leaves
lettuce leaves, to serve
chopped spring onions and Chilli
  Flower, see page 30, to garnish

1 Heat a wok, add beef and dry-fry for about 2 minutes until tender. Transfer to a bowl.

2 In a small bowl, mix together fish sauce, lime juice and sugar. Pour over warm beef, add rice and toss together. Cover and leave until cold.

3 Add chillies, garlic, mint, lime and basil leaves to bowl and toss ingredients together. Line a plate with lettuce leaves and spoon beef mixture into centre. Scatter over spring onions and garnish with a chilli flower.

NUTRITIONAL INFORMATION	
Kcal	190
Protein	25g
Carbs	11g
Fat	5g
Salt	1.1g
Sodium	450mg

Pork & Bamboo Shoot Salad

[SERVES 3–4]

3 tablespoons vegetable oil
3 cloves garlic, chopped
1 small onion, thinly sliced
225 g/8 oz lean pork, very finely
    chopped
1 egg, beaten
225 g/8 oz tin bamboo shoots,
    drained and cut into strips
1 tablespoon fish sauce
1 teaspoon crushed palm sugar
3 tablespoons lime juice
freshly ground black pepper
lettuce leaves, to serve

1 In a wok, heat 2 tablespoons oil, add garlic and onion and cook, stirring occasionally, until lightly browned. Using a slotted spoon, transfer to absorbent kitchen paper to drain; set aside.

2 Add pork to wok and stir-fry for about 3 minutes until cooked through. Using a slotted spoon, transfer to absorbent kitchen paper; set aside. Using absorbent kitchen paper, wipe out wok.

3 Heat remaining oil, pour in egg to make a thin layer and cook for 1–2 minutes until just set. Turn egg over and cook for 1 minute more. Remove egg from wok and roll up. Cut across into strips. In a bowl, toss together pork, bamboo shoots and egg. In a small bowl, stir together fish sauce, sugar, lime juice and pepper. Pour over pork mixture and toss. Serve on lettuce leaves and sprinkle with garlic and onion.

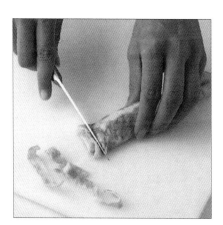

NUTRITIONAL INFORMATION	
Kcal	300
Protein	20g
Carbs	8g
Fat	21g
Salt	1.2g
Sodium	470mg

Chicken & Watercress

[SERVES 3–4]

2 cloves garlic, finely chopped
3-cm/1¹/₂-in piece galangal, finely
  chopped
1 tablespoon fish sauce
3 tablespoons lime juice
1 teaspoon crushed palm sugar
2 tablespoons peanut oil
225 g/8 oz chicken breast meat,
  finely chopped

about 25 dried shrimps
1 bunch watercress, about
  115 g/4 oz, coarse stalks
  removed
3 tablespoons chopped dry-
  roasted peanuts
2 fresh red chillies, seeded and cut
  into fine strips

1 Using a pestle and mortar, pound together garlic and galangal. Mix in fish sauce, lime juice and sugar; set aside. In wok, heat oil, add chicken and stir-fry for about 3 minutes until cooked through.

2 Using a slotted spoon, transfer to absorbent kitchen paper to drain. Put into a serving bowl and set aside.

3 Chop half dried shrimps and add to bowl. Mix in watercress, peanuts and half of chillies. Pour over garlic mixture and toss to mix. Sprinkle with remaining chillies and shrimps.

NUTRITIONAL INFORMATION	
Kcal	370
Protein	36g
Carbs	9g
Fat	21g
Salt	1.2g
Sodium	460mg

Hot Bamboo Shoot Salad

[SERVES 2–3]

1 tablespoon fish sauce
2 tablespoons tamarind water, see page 27
1/2 teaspoon crushed palm sugar
1 clove garlic, finely chopped
1 small fresh red chilli, seeded and finely chopped

175 g/6 oz bamboo shoots, cut into fine strips
1 tablespoon coarsely ground browned rice, see page 27
2 spring onions, including some green part, sliced
coriander leaves, to garnish

1 In a saucepan, heat fish sauce, tamarind water, sugar, garlic, chilli and 2 tablespoons water to the boil.

2 Stir in bamboo shoots and heat for 1–2 minutes.

3 Stir in rice, then turn into a warmed dish, scatter over spring onion and garnish with coriander leaves.

NUTRITIONAL INFORMATION	
Kcal	60
Protein	2g
Carbs	11g
Fat	Trace
Salt	1.4g
Sodium	560mg

Bean Salad

[SERVES 3–4]

2 tablespoons lime juice
2 tablespoons fish sauce
1/2 teaspoon crushed palm sugar
1 1/2 tablespoons Nam Prik, see page 44
2 tablespoons ground roasted peanuts
2 tablespoons vegetable oil

3 cloves garlic, chopped
3 shallots, thinly sliced
1/4 dried red chilli, seeded and finely chopped
2 tablespoons coconut cream, see page 24
225 g/8 oz French beans, very thinly sliced

1 In a small bowl, mix together lime juice, fish sauce, sugar, nam prik, peanuts and 2 tablespoons water; set aside. In a small saucepan, heat oil, add garlic and shallots and cook, stirring occasionally, until beginning to brown.

2 Stir in chilli and cook until garlic and shallots are browned. Using a slotted spoon, transfer to absorbent kitchen paper; set aside.

3 In a small saucepan over a low heat, warm coconut cream, stirring occasionally. Bring a saucepan of water to the boil, add beans, return to the boil and cook for about 30 seconds. Drain and refresh under cold running water. Drain well. Transfer to a serving bowl and toss with shallot mixture and contents of small bowl. Spoon over warm coconut cream.

NUTRITIONAL INFORMATION	
Kcal	230
Protein	8g
Carbs	12g
Fat	16g
Salt	2.8g
Sodium	1100mg

Green Papaya Salad

[SERVES 4–6]

1 small unripe green papaya, peeled and thinly shredded
1 large or 2 small carrots, peeled and thinly shredded
salt and freshly ground black pepper
few lettuce leaves
1 tablespoon crushed roasted peanuts, to garnish

DRESSING:
1 clove garlic, chopped
1 shallot, chopped
2 small red or green chillies, seeded and chopped
1 tablespoon dried shrimps, soaked and rinsed
2 teaspoons palm sugar
3 tablespoons lime juice or vinegar
2 tablespoons fish sauce

1 Mix the shredded papaya and carrot with salt and pepper. Arrange a bed of lettuce leaves on a serving dish and pile the papaya and carrot on top.

2 Using a pestle and mortar, pound the garlic, shallot, chillies, shrimps and sugar to a fine paste. Blend with the lime juice or vinegar and the fish sauce to make the dressing.

3 Garnish the salad with the crushed peanuts and pour the dressing all over it. Do not toss or mix the salad until at the table and ready to serve.

NOTE: This salad can be served either as a starter or as a side dish with main courses.

NUTRITIONAL INFORMATION	
Kcal	60
Protein	3g
Carbs	13g
Fat	Trace
Salt	1.5g
Sodium	580mg

DESSERTS &
DRINKS

Fruit Salad

[SERVES 4–6]

115 g/4 oz crystal sugar
about 350 ml/12 fl oz boiling
   water
1/2 small watermelon or a whole
   honeydew melon
4–5 different fruits (fresh or
   tinned), such as pineapple,
   grapes, lychees, rambutan,
   banana, papaya, mango,
   physallis, star fruit or kiwifruit

1 Make a syrup by dissolving the sugar in the boiling water, then leave to cool.

2 Slice about 7.5 cm/3 in off the top of melon, scoop out flesh, discarding seeds, and cut flesh into small chunks. Prepare all the other fruits by cutting them into small chunks the same size as the melon chunks.

3 Fill melon shell with the fruit and syrup. Cover with clingfilm and chill in the refrigerator for at least 2–3 hours.

NOTE: If using tinned fruit with syrup or natural juice, you can use this instead of making syrup. The nutritional information is based on 850 g/1 lb 14 oz of fruit.

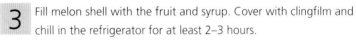

NUTRITIONAL INFORMATION	
Kcal	200
Protein	1g
Carbs	53g
Fat	Trace
Salt	Trace
Sodium	Trace

Coconut Crêpes

[MAKES ABOUT 10]

115 g/4 oz rice flour
85 g/3 oz plain flour
2 tablespoons caster sugar
pinch salt
85 g/3 oz desiccated coconut
2 eggs, beaten
625 ml/20 fl oz coconut milk

green and red food colouring, if
   desired
vegetable oil for frying
mandarin segments, to serve, if
   desired

1 In a bowl, stir together rice flour, sugar, salt and coconut. Form a
well in centre, add egg, then gradually draw in flour, slowly
pouring in coconut milk at same time, to make a smooth batter. If
desired, divide batter evenly between 3 bowls.

2 Stir green food colouring into one bowl to colour batter pale
green; colour another batch pink and leave remaining batch
plain. Heat a 15-cm/6-in crêpe or omelette pan over a moderate heat,
swirl around a little oil, then pour off excess. Stir batter well, then add
2–3 spoonfuls to pan.

3 Rotate to cover base, then cook over moderate heat for about 4
minutes until lightly browned underneath and quite firmly set.
Carefully turn over and cook briefly on other side. Transfer to a warmed
plate and keep warm while cooking remaining batter. Serve rolled up
with mandarin segments, if liked.

NOTE: The mixture is quite delicate and the first few pancakes may be
troublesome.

NUTRITIONAL INFORMATION	
Kcal (Whole recipe)	260
Protein	4g
Carbs	20g
Fat	18g
Salt	Trace
Sodium	Trace

Mango with Sticky Rice

[SERVES 4]

225 g/8 oz sticky rice, soaked
  overnight in cold water
250 ml/8 fl oz coconut milk
pinch salt, to taste
2-4 tablespoons sugar, to taste
2 large ripe mangoes, peeled and
  halved
3 tablespoons coconut cream, see
  page 24
mint leaves to decorate

1 Drain and rinse rice thoroughly. Place in a steaming basket lined with a double thickness of muslin. Steam over simmering water for 30 minutes. Remove from heat.

2 In a bowl, stir together coconut milk, salt and sugar to taste until sugar has dissolved. Stir in warm rice. Set aside for 30 minutes.

3 Thinly slice mangoes by cutting lengthways through flesh to the stone. Discard the stones. Spoon rice into a mound in centre of serving plates and arrange mango slices around. Pour coconut cream over rice. Decorate with mint leaves.

NUTRITIONAL INFORMATION	
Kcal	420
Protein	6g
Carbs	72g
Fat	12g
Salt	Trace
Sodium	Trace

Coconut Custards

[SERVES 4]

3 eggs
2 egg yolks
500 ml/16 fl oz coconut milk
85 g/3 oz caster sugar
few drops rosewater or jasmine
** essence**
toasted coconut, to decorate

1 Preheat the oven to 180C/350F/Gas Mark 4. Place 4 individual heatproof dishes in a baking tin.

2 In a bowl, stir together eggs, egg yolks, coconut milk, sugar and rosewater or jasmine essence until sugar dissolves. Pass through a sieve into dishes. Pour boiling water into baking tin to surround the dishes.

3 Cook in oven for about 20 minutes until custards are lightly set in centre. Remove from baking tin and allow to cool slightly before unmoulding. Serve warm or cold. Decorate with coconut.

NUTRITIONAL INFORMATION	
Kcal	400
Protein	10g
Carbs	25g
Fat	29g
Salt	0.2g
Sodium	70mg

Green & White Jellies

[SERVES 4–6]

3 teaspoons powdered gelatine
5 tablespoons caster sugar
200 ml/7 fl oz coconut milk
85 ml/3 fl oz coconut cream, see
  page 24
2 pieces pandanus leaf, each 7.5
  cm/3 in long, or $^3/_4$–1 teaspoon
  kewra water
green food colouring

(If pandanus leaf or kewra water
  are unavailable, flavour with
  rosewater and colour pink with
  red food colouring, to make Pink
  & White Jellies)

1 Sprinkle 1$^1/_2$ teaspoons gelatine over 1$^1/_2$ tablespoons water in a small bowl and leave to soften for 5 minutes. Stand bowl in a small saucepan of hot water and stir until dissolved. Remove from heat.

2 Put half the sugar and all coconut milk into a medium saucepan and heat gently, stirring until sugar has dissolved. Remove from heat and stir in coconut cream. Stir a little into dissolved gelatine, then stir back into pan. Divide between individual moulds. Set in refrigerator. Put remaining sugar in a medium saucepan with 315 ml/10 fl oz water and pandanus leaf or kewra water.

3 Heat gently, stirring, until sugar dissolves. Bring to the boil, simmer for 2–3 minutes, cover and remove from heat. Set aside for 15 minutes, then remove pandanus leaf, if used. Dissolve remaining gelatine in same way. Stir in a little pandanus liquid, then stir back into medium pan. Add food colouring. Set aside until cold but not set, then pour over set coconut mixture. Place in refrigerator to set. Dip moulds into hot water for 1–2 seconds, then turn out onto cold plates.

NUTRITIONAL INFORMATION	
Kcal	200
Protein	4g
Carbs	21g
Fat	11g
Salt	Trace
Sodium	Trace

Lychee Sorbet

[SERVES 4]

450 g/1 lb fresh lychees in their
  shells or 175 g/6 oz tinned
  lychees, drained
150 g/5 oz caster sugar
300 ml/10 fl oz water
fresh mint sprigs, to decorate

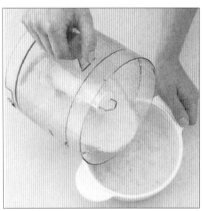

1 Peel fresh lychees, if using and stone them. Heat water and dissolve sugar. When sugar is dissolved, boil for 1 minute. Allow syrup to cool.

2 Place the lychees in a food processor or blender with the syrup and process to a smooth purée.

3 Pour the purée into a freezerproof container and place in the freezer for about 2 hours until almost set. Break up the iced mixture and whip until smooth. Return mixture to the freezer for 30–45 minutes to set until solid. Serve the sorbet decorated with mint leaves.

VARIATION: 2 teaspoons grated root ginger can be added to the sorbet mixture before blending, if desired.

NUTRITIONAL INFORMATION	
Kcal	60
Protein	Trace
Carbs	16g
Fat	0g
Salt	Trace
Sodium	Trace

Lychees in Coconut Custard

[SERVES 4]

3 egg yolks
3–4 tablespoons caster sugar
200 ml/7 fl oz coconut milk
85 ml/3 fl oz coconut cream, see
   page 24
about 1 tablespoon triple distilled
   rose water
red food colouring, if desired
about 16 fresh lychees, peeled,
   halved and stones removed
rose petals, to decorate

1 In a bowl, whisk together egg yolks and sugar. In a medium, preferably non-stick, saucepan, heat coconut milk to just below boiling point, then slowly stir into bowl. Return to pan and cook very gently, stirring with a wooden spoon, until custard coats the back of the spoon.

2 Remove from heat and stir in coconut cream, rose water to taste and sufficient red food colouring to colour, if desired. Leave until cold, stirring occasionally.

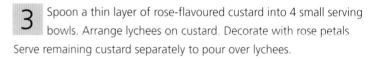

3 Spoon a thin layer of rose-flavoured custard into 4 small serving bowls. Arrange lychees on custard. Decorate with rose petals Serve remaining custard separately to pour over lychees.

NUTRITIONAL INFORMATION	
Kcal	250
Protein	4g
Carbs	24g
Fat	15g
Salt	Trace
Sodium	Trace

Golden Threads

[SERVES 4]

6 egg yolks
1 teaspoon egg white
450 g/1 lb sugar
few drops jasmine essence

1 Strain egg yolks through muslin into a small bowl. Beat lightly with egg white. In a saucepan, gently heat sugar, jasmine essence and 250 ml/8 fl oz water, stirring until sugar dissolves, then boil until thickened slightly. Adjust heat so syrup is hot but not moving.

2 Spoon a small amount of egg yolk into a piping bag fitted with a very fine nozzle or a cone of greaseproof paper with a very small hole in the pointed end. Using a circular movement, carefully dribble a trail into the syrup, making swirls with about a 4–5 cm/1$^1/_2$–2 inch diameter and with a small hole in the centre. Make a few at a time, cooking each briefly until set.

3 Using a skewer inserted in the hole in the centre of the spiral, transfer each nest to a plate. Continue making similar nests with remaining egg yolks. When nests are cool, arrange on a serving plate.

NUTRITIONAL INFORMATION	
Kcal	540
Protein	4g
Carbs	118g
Fat	8g
Salt	Trace
Sodium	16mg

Thai Sweetmeats

[MAKES ABOUT 16]

55 g/2 oz split mung beans, rinsed
45 g/1½ oz desiccated coconut
1 egg
115 g/4 oz palm sugar, crushed
few drops jasmine essence

1 Put mung beans into a medium saucepan, add sufficient water to cover by 4 cm/1½ in. Bring to the boil, then simmer for about 30–45 minutes until tender. Drain through a strainer, then mash thoroughly.

2 Using your fingers, mix in coconut and egg to make a firm paste. Divide into pieces about the size of a small walnut and shape into egg-shaped balls using a spoon. Put sugar into a saucepan, add 185 ml/6 fl oz water and heat gently, stirring, until sugar has dissolved. Bring to the boil. Add jasmine essence to taste and keep hot.

3 Lower each ball into into syrup. Cook for 2–3 minutes. Using a slotted spoon, transfer to a plate. When all sweetmeats have been cooked, spoon over a little syrup. Leave sweetmeats until cold. Sprinkle with a little desiccated coconut to serve.

NUTRITIONAL INFORMATION	
Kcal	60
Protein	1g
Carbs	9g
Fat	2g
Salt	Trace
Sodium	Trace

Limeade

[MAKES ABOUT 1 LITRE/35 FL OZ]

6 limes
115 g/4 oz sugar
700 ml/24 fl oz boiling water
pinch salt
lime slices, to serve

1 Cut each lime in half and squeeze juice.

2 Place skins in a jug, then stir in sugar followed by boiling water. Cover and leave for 15 minutes.

3 Stir in salt. Strain into another jug and add lime juice. Leave to cool, then cover and chill. Serve over ice with lime slices.

NUTRITIONAL INFORMATION	
Kcal (Whole recipe)	500
Protein	2g
Carbs	130g
Fat	0g
Salt	2.0g
Sodium	800mg

Index